CHILDREN OF POVERTY

STUDIES ON THE EFFECTS OF SINGLE PARENTHOOD, THE FEMINIZATION OF POVERTY, AND HOMELESSNESS

edited by

STUART BRUCHEY
ALLAN NEVINS PROFESSOR EMERITUS
COLUMBIA UNIVERSITY

A GARLAND SERIES

OUT HERE BY OURSELVES

THE STORIES OF YOUNG PEOPLE WHOSE MOTHERS HAVE AIDS

DIANE DUGGAN

GARLAND PUBLISHING, INc.
NEW YORK & LONDON / 2000

Published in 2000 by
Garland Publishing Inc.
Garland is an imprint of the Taylor & Francis Group
19 Union Square West
New York, NY 10003

10 9 8 7 6 5 4 3 2 1

Library of Congress Cataloging-in-Publication Data
Duggan, Diane.
    Out here by ourselves : the stories of young people whose mothers
  have AIDS / Diane Duggan.
        p. cm. — (Children of poverty)
    Includes bibliographical references and index.
    ISBN 0-8153-3621-7 (alk. paper)
    1. Children of AIDS patients—Interviews. 2. AIDS (Disease)—
  Patients—Family relationships. 3. Mothers. I. Title. II. Series.
  RA644.A25 D838 2000
  362.1'969792—dc21   00-035376

Printed on acid-free, 250-year-life paper
Manufactured in the United States of America

Contents

Appendices   155

Acknowledgments

I would like to thank the three young people who participated in this study for sharing their experiences with me. I hope that the study will in some small measure alert others to their struggle and perhaps provide some direction as to how best to assist AIDS affected young people towards a more hopeful and satisfying future.

I thank my Dissertation Committee members for helping me through this long undertaking. I appreciate Margot Ely for her passion, depth of knowledge and hard work and for introducing me to so many creative possibilities from which to develop this study. I'm grateful to Gil Trachtman for his sage advice and his thoroughness in helping me to anticipate all the vicissitudes of this process. I'm appreciative of their ability to blend their very different talents to make such a smooth journey for me.

Thank you to Mark Henderson at Garland Publishing for his advice and support in the production of this book.

Thank you to my Dissertation Support Group: Ellen Margolin, Jane Martin, Michelle Bellavita and Judith Evans, for sharing their opinions and insights, as well as for their practical help.

I thank "Sarah" for her generosity in helping me to recruit participants as well as for her courage and steadfastness in aiding young people in trouble and helping recovering substance abusers gain control of their lives.

Last, but certainly not least, I thank my family for their love, understanding and patience throughout this long, sometimes arduous undertaking. Thank you Jude for taking care of the children those many Saturdays and Sundays so I could work. Thank you Aisha and Umar for being the wonderful, loving people you've grown to be.

Out Here By Ourselves

CHAPTER I

Purpose of the Study

INTRODUCTION

The worldwide epidemic of Acquired Immune Deficiency Syndrome (AIDS) is one of the most important public health issues of our time. AIDS was first reported in the United States by the Centers for Disease Control (CDC) on June 5, 1981. Since then the number of people with AIDS has increased geometrically, as has the number of deaths from AIDS, prompting the CDC to note, "The recognition of a disease and its emergence as a leading cause of death within the same decade is without precedent" (CDC, 1992a p. 125). As of May 1999, the cumulative number of AIDS cases in the United States reported to the CDC is 688,200. Of these, 410,800 have died (CDC, 1999). Although protease inhibitors have extended the lives of many people with AIDS (CDC, 1996), slowing the increase in morbidity, not everyone is able to use these medications, and the number of deaths from AIDS remains high.

AIDS is a syndrome which is caused by the Human Immunodeficiency Virus (HIV). When people are infected with HIV they are initially asymptomatic. The virus gradually destroys their immune system, and, until the advent of protease inhibitors in 1995 (CDC, 1996), in the majority of cases HIV developed into AIDS within approximately eight years (Needle, Leach, & Graham-Tomasi, 1989).

At the beginning of the AIDS epidemic in the U.S. the news media focused almost exclusively on the devastation of the gay male community. Only later was the effect of AIDS on heterosexuals in general and women in particular given attention. By 1997 women accounted for 20% of new AIDS cases, compared to 13% in 1992 and 6% in 1982. Even more significantly, while deaths from AIDS in 1996 decreased 15% for men, they increased 3% for women (CDC, 1997a).

Most women with AIDS are of childbearing age, and many of them are single mothers. Sometimes HIV was transmitted to their unborn babies. These infants with AIDS received considerable attention from the news media and from the medical and social service communities because of their urgent needs.

The majority of children of women with AIDS are not infected by HIV, but they are profoundly affected by the illness and in many cases the death of their mothers. Estimates in the mid 1990's predicted that between 72,000 and 125,000 (Levine & Stein, 1994) or 125,000 to 150,000 (Geballe, Gruendel & Andiman, 1995) children would be orphaned by the death of their mother from AIDS by the year 2000. In addition, 60,000 young people over the age of 18 would have lost their mother to AIDS (Levine & Stein). A United Nations report estimated that in December, 1999 there were 70,000 children in North American who had been orphaned by AIDS. This figure counts only HIV negative children under the age of fifteen (Altman, 1999). Despite their numbers and the worldwide attention given to AIDS, the plight of non-infected children and adolescents who are affected by AIDS through the illness and death of their parents has been virtually disregarded (Dane & Miller, 1992). Dr. Peter Piot, the head of the United Nations World AIDS Day program stated that children orphaned by AIDS are "the most forgotten aspect of the AIDS epidemic" (Altman. p. 28).

The experience and needs of AIDS affected children and youth demand attention. Adolescents and young adults are of particular concern because many young people are sexually active and therefore at risk for contracting HIV themselves. Most do not regularly use condoms (Flora & Thoresen, 1988), the only form of contraception to offer any protection against HIV. The prevalence of unprotected sex among American adolescents is demonstrated in their rather dramatic statistics for sexually transmitted diseases (STDs). Three million adolescents annually contract a sexually transmitted disease (Sexuality Information and Education Council of the United States [SIECUS], 1997). The presence of an STD not only indicates the possibility that HIV could have been transmitted as well, it actually facilitates the transmission of HIV (SIECUS). The long latency period before HIV infection causes the symptoms of AIDS makes it likely that infections incurred during adolescence will be diagnosed as AIDS in young adulthood. This risk is borne out in the fact that to date 107,281 people in the 20–29 year old age range have been diagnosed with AIDS (CDC, 1997b).

RESEARCH QUESTIONS

Very little is known about the impact of a mother's illness or death from AIDS on their adolescent and young adult children. This study attempts to discover through the personal stories of a small number of participants the issues and concerns most relevant to their experience. Qualitative methodology allowed the participants to respond in their own terms, so that I could elicit and explore those issues which were most important to the young people themselves. I recursively analyzed the information they provided to guide the course of the research while it was in progress. The study sought answers from the perspectives of three young people to the following initial research questions:

- What is the experience of adolescents and young adults who have a family member with AIDS?
- What impact does this experience have on their feelings about themselves and on their behavior?

A key characteristic of the qualitative method is that the questions for study evolve as the research progresses (Ely, 1991; Bogden & Bicklen, 1982; Lincoln & Guba, 1985). The initial questions became more specific and focused, based on the issues brought up by the young people who participated in the study. Since all three participants had mothers who had AIDS, I focused on that situation. When issues about the instability of their lives, having babies, and their relationships with their mothers emerged as prominent for the young people, I focused further inquiry on those areas.

CHAPTER II

Background

INTRODUCTION

Most of the extensive literature on adolescents and AIDS focuses on prevention. It is only within the past few years that the situation of adolescents affected by AIDS in the family has begun to be looked at, usually in conjunction with preadolescent children in families with AIDS.

Dimensions of the Problem

The Orphan Project ((Levine & Stein, 1994) developed an epidemiological model to estimate the number of children and youth orphaned by the AIDS epidemic. The model was applied to five cities with the highest rates of HIV infections. Together these urban areas account for 60% of AIDS cases in the United States. Based on that model, it is predicted that by the year 2000 between 72,000 and 125,000 American children and youth will have lost their mother to AIDS. An additional 60,000 young adults of eighteen and older will also have lost their mothers.

The Centers for Disease Control and Prevention places the numbers for children orphaned by the AIDS epidemic in the United States at 125,000 to 150,000 (Geballe, Gruendel & Andiman). Although these estimates are higher, the CDC considers them to be conservative. Approximately three quarters of these AIDS affected children and youth are uninfected by the virus. In December of 1999 the United Nations estimated the number of children in North American orphaned by AIDS at 70,000. This figure includes only HIV negative children under the age of fifteen (Altman, 1999).

New York City has the highest rate of HIV infection in the country, and predictions for its population of AIDS orphans are more than four times greater than those of the next most affected city. The medium range estimate of the

7

number of children and adolescents in New York City who will lose their mothers to AIDS by the year 2000 are 15,000 children and 15,000 adolescents, for a total of 30,000 motherless children and teens (Levine & Stein). According to *The New York Times*, there are already 30,000 uninfected minor children of mothers who died from AIDS in New York City, and that figure is expected to rise to 50,000 by the year 2001 (Richardson, 1998). *The Times* also reported that AIDS is the leading cause of death for mothers of children under eighteen in New York State.

The needs of the Orphan Project's estimated 60,000 young adults of eighteen years or older who will also lose their mothers to AIDS by the year 2000 may seem less compelling because of their age. However they also face serious psychosocial, economic and legal problems, and they may not yet be ready to live on their own. Most of the orphaned children and youth are not themselves HIV infected, but they are severely affected by the illness and death of their mother from AIDS.

The epidemiological model developed by the Orphan Project is represented schematically as an iceberg. At the tip of the iceberg are the most noticeable members of AIDS affected families, the 6,000 pediatric AIDS cases in the U.S. which had been reported to the CDC at the time of their study. These children receive the most attention from the public and from medical and social service professionals because of their urgent needs. Since most of these children acquired HIV perinatally rather than through their own voluntary behavior they also generate the most sympathy from the public. Just below the iceberg's tip of reported pediatric AIDS cases are the known cases of HIV infected children and adolescents who have not yet developed AIDS. There are many more cases of known pediatric HIV infection than full blown AIDS cases, over 300% more in 1989 (Levine & Stein). The next portion of the iceberg represents the uninfected siblings of the group with AIDS or HIV infection. These children and youth were either born before their mother became infected or were born to HIV infected women but escaped maternal transmission of the virus, which occurs in less than one-third of births to HIV+ women (Levine & Stein). The largest and most hidden part of the iceberg model includes the uninfected children and adolescents whose parent, other adult relative or committed caregiver is either living with AIDS or has died of the disease but who do not have an HIV infected sibling.

The epidemiological models for projecting the numbers of AIDS orphans focus on motherless youngsters because the overwhelming majority of caregiving parents who die of AIDS are mothers. There are few data on the offspring of men who die of AIDS, and there are no models for men comparable to fertility rates of women, which would allow statisticians to estimate the numbers of children and youth affected by the death of a father from AIDS. If there were, it would only add to the staggering numbers of youngsters affected by the death of a mother from AIDS.

Family Demographics

Since 1986 AIDS has been the leading cause of death for New York City women between the ages of fifteen and forty-four (Cohen, 1993). African-American and Hispanic women have been disproportionately affected by AIDS in the United States (Henggeler, Melton & Rodrigue, 1992). Although they constitute only 19% of all women nationally, 73% of women in the United States with AIDS are Black or Hispanic (Ibid.). The latest statistics for New York City show that women of color account for an even higher proportion of women diagnosed with AIDS, with African-American women accounting for 53% and Latinas for 34% of all cases of AIDS in women (NYCDOH, April, 1997).

The two most common vectors for HIV transmission in women are injecting drug use and heterosexual intercourse with an HIV infected partner (Cohen). The more efficient blood to blood transmission through needles used to inject drugs accounts for the majority of cases of AIDS in women. Overall in the United States, injecting drug use is implicated in 71% of AIDS cases in women (Barth, Pietrzak & Ramler, 1993).

The literature on families of parents with AIDS reflects these demographics. The New York City Human Resources Administration Division of AIDS Services (DAS) conducted face to face interviews with adolescents and parents in AIDS affected families, using their own questionnaire and several quantitative measures to assess the mental health needs of well adolescents (Draimin, Hudis & Segura, 1992). They looked at a sample of forty families headed by a parent with AIDS. In 90% of the families this was the mother, and she had either a past or current history of drug abuse. 42% of the families in the study were African-American and 58% were Latino. This largely reflected the demographics of the agency's caseload in 1991–1992, which was 91% Latino and African-American.

Project Talk is a New York City based program designed to increase coping and parenting skills of parents with AIDS. They gathered data on 151 of their participating AIDS affected families. 38% of the families were African-American and 47% were Hispanic. Again most of the infected parents were mothers and most had a past or current history of injecting drug use (Rotheram-Borus, 1995). Similarly, the clinicians at Columbia Presbyterian's HIV Center for Clinical and Behavioral Studies reported that most AIDS affected families at their center were African-American or Latino (Mellins, 1995).

Issues of ethnicity may affect the response of families to the stresses of coping with AIDS. For example, a family's relationship with the health care system can be greatly influenced by ethnicity (Groce, 1995). "There is sufficient historical justification for the expectation of prejudice/racism towards minority group members in the area of health care. These expectations exist at both an individual and a community/public action level" (DesJarlais, Casriel, Stepherson & Friedman, 1990, p. 5). Many African-Americans distrust the health care system and point to the infamous Tuskeegee Syphilis Experiment as confirmation for their fears (Fernando, 1993). An early myth about AIDS, told to me by several teenagers who are not included in this study, is that HIV was created by U.S. government scientists and purposely introduced into the African-American community to exterminate Black people.

Most of the heads of families with AIDS are single women. Their diagnosis tends to come later in the course of their illness, and they usually die far sooner after the diagnosis than men with AIDS (Cohen). The stresses of caring for a family, the poverty and prejudice many of them suffer, and for many, a history of drug abuse may further compromise their fragile health and affect their ability to access appropriate medical care.

The fact that intravenous drug use figures prominently in the histories of the majority of these families can also have a profound influence on the families' ability to cope with the crisis of AIDS. Many users of illegal drugs distrust "the system" and may avoid encounters with medical and social service personnel because they may fear being reported to child welfare or law enforcement (Barth, Pietrzak & Ramler, 1993). The parent-child relationship is likely to have suffered throughout the course of the parent's drug addiction. The need to acquire and inject drugs and the varying ability to cope with routine tasks while under their influence are overwhelming organizers of a drug addict's day. Although most drug dependent mothers express concern for the welfare of their children, they often experience difficulties in adequately caring for them (Ibid.). When a woman is abusing drugs her behavior may be impulsive, aggressive, and self-destructive. Her anxiety and low tolerance for frustration, as well as a compelling, self-absorbed quest for drugs can lead her to abuse or neglect her children. Women who have experienced discrimination based on their past or current drug use may be more reluctant to reveal their AIDS diagnosis to their children because they fear anger and accusations of blame from them (Draimin et al). Often the mother's family of origin has cut its ties with her because of her drug abuse (Barth et al.). This lack of contact with the extended family can further constrict the support network available to her children during times of crisis.

Another demographic aspect of AIDS is that it is not distributed uniformly throughout the population but is highly localized. It tends to thrive where there is a concentration of other social ills (National Research Council, 1993). With the exception of the gay community, the communities where AIDS is most prevalent suffer from a "synergism of plagues" (Wallace, 1988): poverty, neglect, high levels of substance abuse, and family and community violence. All of these characteristics make coping with the disease far more difficult for the AIDS affected families who live in them. At least 80% of AIDS affected children and youth come from poor, minority communities. The iceberg metaphor of the Orphan Project's epidemiological model is tossed about in a "stormy sea of violence, homelessness, drug and alcohol use, poverty, discrimination, and community disintegration" (Levine & Stein. p. 12).

CHARACTERISTICS OF AIDS AFFECTED YOUTH

Many factors influence a young person's reaction to the death of a parent. Whatever the cause of death, a conflicted relationship with the ill parent can adversely influence the outcome for the youngster. In the case of AIDS there are other factors that can exacerbate the situation. AIDS generally runs a protracted, erratic course filled with uncertainty as to when the next opportunistic infection will strike, the nature and duration of that affliction, and whether the person will survive. There are periods of relative health punctuated by awful and sometimes disfiguring symptoms, such as profound weakness, severe and prolonged diarrhea, visible skin lesions, and wasting. Youngsters living at home witness the suffering and deterioration of their parent, and the household must revolve around his or her health care needs. This creates prolonged and inescapable stress within the family, culminating in what was an inevitable and often grueling death (Lewis, 1995). Protease inhibitors have changed this outlook for many people with AIDS, but these drugs do not work for everyone, and they may be withheld from patients, such as drug abusers, whose lifestyle is judged by doctors as too chaotic to sustain the exacting regimens these medicines require (Sontag & Richardson, 1997).

The DAS study (Draimin et al.) focused specifically on the mental health needs of adolescents whose parent(s) had AIDS, and their findings were grim. Adolescents in the study had experienced multiple losses in their lives apart from their current AIDS crisis. These losses may have included the death or incarceration of a significant person in their lives and the divorce or separation of their parents. Many of the youth were isolated and did not have a best friend. The stigma of AIDS in the family compounded this isolation, as did moving, with or without the rest of the household. Custody arrangements were problematic for all families, but a problem particular to older teens was the refusal of potential caregivers to take responsibility for them, even when they would accept younger children. This was often due to the difficult, acting out behavior many of these young people displayed. Almost three-quarters of the teens were experiencing problems in school, and twenty-five percent of the adolescent boys had had recent brushes with law enforcement.

Early analysis of an on-going study of adolescents in families with AIDS in New York City showed that within the past six months 72% reported being involved in a serious physical fight, 13% had been arrested or gone to court for illegal activity and 2% had gone to jail (Hudis, 1995).

The older teens in the DAS study, from ages seventeen to nineteen, had different issues than the younger teens and children. The researchers found them more difficult to contact and engage. Often these teens were living away from home, sometimes on the street. They had either left home or "were in such conflict with adult authority figures that they were frequently moving from one living situation to another" (p. 7). This parallels the situation of the teens I interviewed, as well as those who were unavailable for my study because of their extremely unstable living situations.

Some older teens could not be located for the DAS study. The researchers felt these young people experienced the greatest difficulty coping with their parent's illness and death and the resulting changes in their living situation. If there was a custody plan at all, it hadn't worked out, or they had made a poor adjustment to the demands of their new living situation. These youth moved in with friends or distant relatives, or they lived on the street.

The youth in the DAS study often acted out in very self-destructive ways. The team defined acting out as truancy, arrest or probation, suspension from school, and defiance of parental rule setting, including staying out all night or being out of touch for days at a time. Parents described their increasing difficulty supervising those youth who remained at home. This was partly due to their increasing incapacitation from AIDS, but there was another dimension. Because of their impending death parents expressed reluctance to jeopardize their relationship with their adolescent children by disciplining them.

Youth who had already lost their parent to AIDS told researchers that they wanted to do well in school because it had been important to their late mothers that they graduate. However, most of these young people experienced significant problems at school. Again, the most serious instances in this study were among older teens, whose fighting and seriously disruptive behavior resulted in suspensions from school and in some cases referrals to restrictive special education programs based on their behavior problems. Some students dropped out, especially girls who were pregnant.

Lewis, writing from a psychodynamic perspective on the issues of uninfected children and youth in AIDS affected families (1995) notes that adolescence is a time when young people must deal with separating from their parents and resolving ambivalent feelings towards them, establishing mature relationships (including sexual ones) with others, attaining mastery over their body and their impulses, and redefining their identity in the context of these changes. Ambivalent feelings towards the parent with AIDS may be expressed in severe behavior problems. The intensity of the ambivalence may make normal separation from the parent almost impossible and lead to impulsive "solutions" such as extreme defiance of parental authority or running away. Some maladaptive defense mechanisms employed by youth, such as identification, projection and acting out may cause a teen to put him/herself in the place of the ill parent and behave as though harming him/herself can protect the parent from harm. Anxiety about the parent and the teen's own risk of contracting AIDS may lead to counterphobic risk-taking, including high-risk sexual behavior and drug abuse.

In her case study of two adolescent survivors of parents with AIDS, Demb noted that their behavior was characterized by "risk taking, depression and sexual acting out" (1989, p. 343). One of the teens spoke of her fear of condoms, which in her mind caused AIDS rather than prevented the disease. This attitude doubtlessly compounded her risk for contracting AIDS or another sexually transmitted disease. Both teens in the study had had multiple losses and lacked a supportive social network, partly due to the circumstances of living with drug abusing, terminally ill parents.

Behavioral Symptoms and Issues of Psychopathology

The DAS study used several quantitative measures of symptomatology, such as the parent version of the Child Behavior Checklist (Achenbach, 1978), the Children's Depression Inventory (Kovacs, 1983), and the Spielberger State Trait Anxiety Index for Youth (Spielberger, 1983). The Child Behavior Checklist showed a predominance of externalizing symptoms, but the majority of the young people did not meet the criteria for clinical severity. The researchers, who had also interviewed the teens felt that although they did not exhibit frank psychopathology, they were greatly distressed by their situation.

The two groups of adolescents in the DAS study, those whose parent was living with AIDS and those whose parent had died, did not differ significantly from each other or from national norms on the scales of depression or anxiety. However, both the parents and the researchers felt that the adolescents were exhibiting depressive symptoms. The researchers, whose impressions were that 58% of the youth were clinically depressed, remarked on the fact that the assessment instruments were not able to capture the anxiety and pain they felt from the young people during their structured interviews. They theorized that perhaps the coping mechanisms used by the families to deal with their situation, including the acting out of the teenagers, kept their vulnerabilities hidden from the reach of the psychometric instruments, if not from the sensitivities of the interviewers. This contrast suggests that the open ended interview format, with its human contact and depth of inquiry, can afford greater sensitivity to the emotional state of the research participants.

Clinicians at Columbia Presbyterian's HIV Center for Clinical and Behavioral Studies treat children and adolescents from AIDS affected families who have been diagnosed with a mental disorder. Of 194 youngsters served by the clinic they reported 50% were diagnosed with Adjustment Disorders, 26% with Attention Deficit Hyperactive Disorder, 11% with Oppositional Defiant or Conduct Disorder, and 27% with a Learning Disability. Over 50% of the youngsters had at least two psychiatric diagnoses (Mellins, 1995).

Dane (1994) reports that some AIDS orphans show symptoms of post traumatic stress disorder. However, she notes that for the most part they should be considered highly vulnerable, rather than ill or disturbed. This might only add a new stigma and hinder them in their efforts to rebuild their identities and their lives.

Adolescent Risk Behaviors

Adolescents who engage in unprotected sexual activity are significantly at risk for contracting HIV. At present a small but significant and steadily growing percentage of teens present with the symptoms of full-blown AIDS (CDC, 1997b). However, the risk is borne out in the fact that people in the 20–29 year old age range constitute 21% of AIDS cases (Ibid.). Given the long latency period before HIV develops into AIDS, it is likely that many of these young adults acquired the virus when they were adolescents (Brooks-Gunn, Boyer & Hein, 1988).

A study of Job Corps applicants between 1987 and 1990 showed that one in 278 of these mostly disadvantaged youth was infected with HIV. An alarmingly higher rate was found among African-American and Hispanic applicants from the Northeast, with one out of every forty infected (St. Louis, Conway, Hayman, Miller, Petersen & Donders, 1991).

There are many efforts to design and implement sex education and risk reduction programs to help adolescents protect themselves from acquiring HIV through unprotected sex (Britton, 1992; Brooks-Gunn et al.; Brown & Fritz, 1988; Flora &Thoresen, 1988; Morales & Bok, 1992; Patierno, 1991). Some of these efforts target specific high risk groups of teens (Martin & Hetrick, 1987; Rotheram-Borus, Koopman & Bradley, 1988; Hein, 1990), but there are no programs designed to meet the needs of AIDS affected adolescents and youth. Findings from homeless and street youth are relevant to AIDS affected young people because of the severe housing difficulties of older youth in AIDS affected families. AIDS is more common in homeless and street youths. One center in New York City serving homeless youth reported that 7% of the youth they worked with were HIV+ (Hein).

The Orphan Project noted that teens affected by AIDS in the family are more prone to exhibit multiple behavioral problems as well as to engage in behaviors which put them at increased risk for contracting HIV themselves (Levine & Stein). Sixteen of the older adolescents in the DAS study filled out self-report questionnaire on their sexual activity and their own drug use. Nine reported having had sexual intercourse at least once. Four out of the five girls who responded had been pregnant at least once, and one out of the four boys had fathered a child. Only three of the young people reported using marijuana. It is very difficult to get good data on intimate or illicit activities such as sexual behavior and drug use through a questionnaire. In my experience in the interviews for my study, the young people initially denied engaging in unprotected sex and using drugs. They seemed reticent to acknowledge "wrongdoing" to an adult. It was only after more discussion that they admitted to these behaviors, and even then they couched their admission with qualifications as to the limited extent of the behavior and justifications for these lapses. This observation highlights the benefits of using a qualitative approach in exploring issues such as sexual behavior and drug use "to provide information of a sensitive nature that cannot usually be uncovered in surveys or formal interviews" (Herdt & Boxer, p. 172). Given the limitations of gathering this type of information with surveys, the data from the small sample of self report respondents in the DAS study showed a very high percent of the teens were engaging in high risk activities. 75% of the young women in her small sample were evidently engaging in unprotected sex.

Many sexually active teens suffer lapses in following safer sex practices. However, the enormous, unrelenting cumulative stresses faced by AIDS affected teens may make them more likely to engage in high risk behavior than their unaffected peers. The death of a parent by itself is one of the most potent factors in predicting maladaptive outcome (Brooks-Gunn et al.). In addition, young people in AIDS affected families face multiple stresses, including the stigma of the disease, the secrecy around discussing it in the family and especially outside the family, poverty, past or current drug abuse, fear for the future, and the awful pain of witnessing the deterioration and eventual death of their mother. Some teens turn to drug use as a way of escaping unpleasant feelings (Draimin et al.). However, drugs create their own problems because they are illegal and cause impaired judgment, which can lead to other risky behaviors, including unprotected sex. Problem behaviors tend to cluster, and individuals exhibiting risky sexual behavior and drug use are also more likely to be anxious, depressed, have problems in school and with law enforcement, and to attempt suicide (Ensminger, 1990).

It has been argued that knowing a person with AIDS can deter teens from engaging in risky sexual behaviors. The conventional wisdom was that if only teens knew someone with AIDS, they would take the threat of the disease seriously and take measures to protect themselves from contracting HIV, either through abstaining from sex or practicing safer sex (Yondorf, 1990). Zimet et al. began with the hypothesis that adolescents would be more concerned about their vulnerability to AIDS if they knew someone with the disease. They explored the effect of teens knowing someone with AIDS on their reluctance to interact with people known to have AIDS and their worries about their personal vulnerability to HIV infection (Zimet, Hillier, Anglin, Ellich, Krowchuk, & Williams, 1991). They found the experience of knowing someone with AIDS reduced irrational fears about interacting with HIV+ individuals, but there was no support for the idea that teens who knew someone with AIDS experienced higher levels of personal vulnerability. Unfortunately they did not include information on the teens' relationship with the person with AIDS.

Depression may make some adolescents more likely to engage in unprotected intercourse or other behaviors that would increase their risk of contracting HIV (Rotheram-Borus, Koopman & Bradley 1988). In view of the findings by Draimin et al. and Demb on the high degree of depression among adolescent offspring of persons with AIDS, this seems to be a very important factor in risky behavior with these youth. Similarly, Hayes (1987) found that low self esteem is linked to decreased use of contraception.

STIGMA

AIDS has a dual stigma within our society, both as a lethal disease and through its identification with groups already stigmatized prior to its advent (Herek & Glunt, 1988). Because AIDS is incurable and transmissible, people with AIDS, by their very existence, are often perceived as putting other people at risk. The deadly nature of the disease and the visible wasting associated with it would likely have caused it to be stigmatized regardless of the population it infected. However, in this country AIDS first emerged among gay males, followed by injecting drug abusers. The fact that these first two waves of the epidemic concentrated on populations that were considered outside the pale of polite society and were themselves already stigmatized considerably increased the negative feelings associated with the disease.

Dane and Miller (1992) discuss three different but interrelated facets of stigma that complicate the mourning of children and adolescents whose parents have died of AIDS. The first is the acceptance and internalization of negative attitudes towards the self, such as damage, inferiority and difference. This changes the way an individual deals with others. The second is the general stigma of a bereaved person as tainted by death. Bereaved adolescents may feel shame and dread returning to school because they do not wish to be questioned by peers. Added to these is the stigma attached to AIDS, which intensifies the trauma experienced by AIDS orphans. Feelings of isolation and estrangement from the peer group which result from AIDS related stigma are particularly painful for adolescents.

Disclosure

The stigma of AIDS is a major factor in the secrecy and denial surrounding the parent's illness. In a symposium on the adaptation of siblings of children with AIDS, Bettoli-Vaughn reported that 70% of siblings in her sample were not told of their mother's AIDS diagnosis and 73% were not told of their ill sibling's diagnosis (1995). Nagler, Adnopoz, & Forsyth (1995) write that "clinical experience strongly suggests that fewer than half of parents in HIV-affected families tell their children about the infection (p. 75). Even when youngsters know their parent's diagnosis they are often constrained from talking to others about it, even to counselors, by feelings of disloyalty and fear of being associated with the stigma of AIDS.

40% of the youth in the DAS study did not know their parent either had AIDS or had died of the disease. Even for those youngsters able to accept the loss of their parent, the shame and guilt associated with AIDS was very difficult to cope with. Almost all the children who did know had been told not to tell anyone outside the family about it. Many of the youth in AIDS affected families were isolated and did not have a best friend. The stigma of AIDS in the family compounded this isolation, and of those who did have a best friend, none had told the best friend that their mother had AIDS.

Disclosure was a big issue in the Project Talk study (Rotheram-Borus, 1995). Only 44% of the parents had disclosed to all their children, and 26% had not disclosed to any. The clinicians noted that teenagers tended to act out more, in terms of more unprotected sex and significantly more sexual partners, if the nature of their mother's illness had been disclosed to them, especially if no custody plans had been made. This finding underscores the importance of thinking through the implications of disclosure and striving to make sure affected youngsters' basic needs for care will be met.

In an effort to respect each family's decision on how to handle disclosure of the parent's AIDS, interviewers in the DAS study avoided using the terms AIDS or HIV unless the interviewee used them. Some families had not disclosed the cause of the parent's illness or death to the teenagers, but many youngsters who had not been told and said they did not know nonetheless had suspicions. Sometimes they found out about their parent's illness because of the taunts of neighbors. Among the adolescents who had been told, many frequently coped with their parent's illness through denial and refused to discuss it or matters related to it.

The authors of the DAS study strongly felt that whether or not to tell the children was a parent's or guardian's prerogative. Disclosure can have many ramifications, and there are legitimate reasons why parents may choose not to reveal the nature of their illness to their children.

Custody

This secrecy and denial surrounding AIDS directly affects custody planning. Oftentimes decisions are delayed because of a parent's inability to accept or disclose their diagnosis. Custody planning for older adolescents is particularly difficult because of their frequently severe acting out behaviors.

The Project Talk study noted that while 83% of parents recognized the need for custody planning, only 24% had discussed it with social service personnel, and then only about their younger children. When plans were made for older children and teens the youngsters had significantly better outcomes in terms of fewer sex partners and less unsafe sexual behaviors.

BEREAVEMENT

Very little work has been done on adolescent bereavement (Hudis, 1995). The little that has been done suggests that bereaved adolescents may be at risk for frequent unprotected sex with multiple partners, behavior problems and substance abuse (Ibid., Ensminger, 1990). To date there have been no controlled, prospective studies on bereaved adolescents who have lost a parent to AIDS (Hudis).

One of the very few investigations of the bereavement of AIDS orphans was done by Dane and Miller (1992). They point out that the death of a parent is a debilitating experience, made even more traumatic by the stigma of AIDS; children and adolescents who lose a parent to AIDS suffer from both grief and trauma. On top of this most of these survivors live in poor communities of color and suffer from poverty and discrimination. A concern for these children and youth is their ability to mourn their loss in a manner which will promote healing and psychological adjustment. They found that the AIDS survivors they observed showed many problems with "cognition (including memory, school performance, and learning), the child's affect, interpersonal relations, impulse control, and vegetative functioning" (p. 66).

Bowlby and Parkes (1979), as cited by Dane and Miller, describe four stages in the grief process. These stages can and often do overlap, but consideration of them helps to highlight some common characteristics of bereavement. The first stage is often denial, which shields the individual from the overwhelming shock of the loved one's death. This is adaptive only in the short term, and reality usually intrudes to diminish this numbness within minutes, hours or days. This is followed by anguish at the separation from the loved one, which may be accompanied by intense physical discomfort. This stage is characterized by yearning and searching for the loved one. The next phase occurs when the individual gives up the search for the deceased and is typified by depression and lack of interest in the future. Thoughts of suicide are most likely in this phase of disorientation and disorganization. The final phase is one of resolution and reorganization, when the mourner has become better able to accept the finality of the loved one's death. Time alone is not a healer. It is necessary to work through the conflicts brought up by death in each stage. If not they may become intensified, more convoluted and harder to resolve.

The DAS researchers saw three distinct stages which teens had to negotiate in coping with their parent's illness and death. In the first stage issues of health concerns, access to health care and disclosure were prominent. In the second stage custody planning and coping with death and dying were of primary importance. In the third stage, after the parent's death, grieving the loss of the parent, working out new family relationships and beginning a new life were the paramount concerns.

It is not uncommon to feel guilt over the death of a loved one. The classic interpretation of guilt following the death of a parent is that it relates to unconscious hostility directed toward the deceased. All children and adolescents harbor angry feelings towards their parents, and the guilt they may feel after their death is not only a reflection of their fear they may have caused the parent's death, but it is also a way to experience a feeling of control in the situation. This is an issue that must be dealt with in bereavement counseling. If allowed to persist, these feelings of guilt can interfere with mourning and can give rise to aggressive acting out and antisocial behavior (Dane & Miller). The issue can be complicated in the case of AIDS deaths because the silence surrounding the death can make survivors more likely to blame themselves. Dane and Miller note that the great majority of children and adolescents in treatment have not talked to anyone else about their reactions to their parent's death.

Adolescents are most vulnerable to problems resulting from arrested grieving. Expressions of anger may afford them a sense of power to counteract feelings of helplessness and the yearning to regress and be taken care of. Adolescent mourning may be complicated by resistance to talking to adults and problems with separation and dependence.

Suicide is an issue, not just in severely depressed youngsters, but also in those who long for a reunion with the parent and think of death as a way to achieve that reunion.

Post-death rituals such as viewing the body, funerals and memorials can provide a forum to express sad feelings, receive condolences from family and the community and begin the work of grief. However, when the death is from AIDS these rituals may be curtailed because of fear of stigmatization and outright discrimination on the part of family, community, funeral directors, and even clergy.

The stigma of AIDS can greatly complicate mourning. Survivors have to cope with rejection and hostility just at the time they are most in need of support (Dane, 1994). The reactions they feel from others may cause them to alter their behavior, keeping their grief, anger and shame inside. This can result in a failure to resolve issues of bereavement. The shame and guilt they feel may promote a tendency to deny the facts of the loved one's death or disavow them, which can provoke guilt. Stigma provokes a "conspiracy of silence" (Ibid.) which can severely impair the youngster's efforts to understand and cope with their loss. To acknowledge a problem is the first step to being able to cope with it.

Expressing sad feelings is an important part of working through grief. However, in the case of AIDS this may be blocked by secrecy and the fear of being associated with the stigma of AIDS. This can result in alternate, maladaptive expression of these feelings behaviorally in disruptive and antisocial conduct and in high-risk behavior (Lewis). Mourning can be further complicated by factors in AIDS affected families such as drug abuse, neglect and abuse.

The exigencies of life in the inner city neighborhoods where AIDS is most common impose their own burdens on families mourning AIDS related deaths. It is difficult to resolve one's grief when other crises demand attention. The AIDS related death itself brings practical and legal issues, such as custody and financial support for the survivors, as well as the emotional upheaval and pain the illness and death cause. Many AIDS orphans have experienced multiple losses, which puts them at increased risk to develop physical and psychological disorders (Dane).

Dane and Miller note that "inner-city residents grieving death from AIDS were frequently inhibited in their mourning" (p. 137) by socioenvironmental factors. Inner city families may need help in overcome bureaucratic red tape and prejudice within the community due to the stigma of AIDS. In addition to facilitating bereavement, professionals need to provide information and support and help to clarify problems and consider solutions. Dane and Miller also recommend that mental health practitioners become sensitive to mourning customs of African-American and Hispanic inner city families. This knowledge can help families to be comforted by their own values and find meaning in the death of their loved one in the context of their religious and spiritual beliefs.

The question of drug abuse further complicates bereavement. In minority communities drug abusers may be seen in two perspectives. From a wider perspective they are the bane of the community, preying on others and casting the entire community in a bad light in the eyes of the outside world. From another, more personal perspective, they may be the children, siblings, or parents of community families, fallen victim to the scourge of drugs. While they may be rejected and vilified in the eyes of the community as a whole, they are often loved and prayed for by their families. This ambivalence adds to the stigma of AIDS and complicates the mourning of survivors after the death of a former drug abuser from AIDS. Survivors need to feel that their loved ones' lives had value and that their own grief is socially recognized. This helps them to find meaning in their pain and to eventually resolve their grief.

When the person who abuses drugs is one's own mother, an additional set of problems must be considered. Often the mother-child relationship is damaged by a mother's drug addiction. She may be emotionally unsupportive, neglectful or abusive. Severe family problems, long-term stress and trauma are likely (Dane). This can damage the youngster's sense of self and ability to form trusting relationships with other adults, which are necessary to cope with the loss of the parent.

NEEDS OF AIDS AFFECTED YOUTH

The DAS study strongly recommended that services for AIDS affected teens should be developed. Among the services needed are supportive counseling, bereavement counseling, and school and court advocates. Counselors should be sensitive to the child's need for privacy. Nagler, Adnopoz & Forsyth (1995) recommend that clinicians working with AIDS affected families extend themselves to the families, perhaps providing services in the home. Repeated home visits and follow-up telephone calls may be necessary after canceled or broken appointments to prove that the clinician can be trusted.

57% of the teens in the DAS study had not received counseling within the previous two years. Of the older adolescents, only one in the study mentioned a school staff member who was aware of their loss, and this was a coach, not a counselor. Three-quarters of the students who had had counseling expressed satisfaction with it. Those who were dissatisfied with counseling felt they had been coerced into going. Two young people had been offered counseling at school but refused because they felt their confidentiality would not be maintained.

Clinicians in the Project Talk study reported that they have a difficult time getting adolescent children of AIDS infected mothers to come to counseling groups. However, when they do come they are able to share and to gain support from others.

CHAPTER III

How the Study Was Conducted

The purpose of this study is to explore the impact on the lives of adolescents and young adults of having a mother who is living with AIDS or who has died of the disease. In order to explore this question I used a qualitative case study methodology, which included conducting in-depth interviews with two adolescents and one twenty year old.

MY STANCE IN THE ROLE OF RESEARCHER

In qualitative methodology the researcher is the main instrument in the collection of data (Bogdan and Bicklen, 1982). It is therefore important to acknowledge the assumptions and biases I bring to the study as a way of mitigating their effect (Ely, 1991).

I approached this study from several different but compatible perspectives. First of all, I consider myself a humanist, and I tend to focus on people's strengths rather than their disabilities. I have been professionally involved in education and special education for the past twenty-five years, much of this time with teenagers. I have learned a great deal from young people by treating them with the same respect I would like accorded to me and by trying my best to listen to what they have to say. I have found this approach to be far more fruitful than focusing on labels or diagnoses.   I am a certified sex educator, and I believe that sexuality is a positive, healthy and potentially enriching aspect of human experience. I taught sexuality to adolescents for several years, and I wrote a short book on the subject for learning disabled teens. I have continued to use this knowledge base in the psychological counseling and group work I currently do with adolescents. My experiences have given me an appreciation for the intensity and pervasive influence of sexuality in the lives of adolescents. This is often a time of great vulnerability and confusion about sexuality, exacerbated by the paucity of frank, sensitive talk about it, as well as by media and peer pressure to engage in sexual activity. I am especially interested in the delicate balance for young people between acknowledging and valuing their sexuality on the one hand and appreciating the need for responsible, life-enhancing sexual behavior on the other.

Although my background as a sex educator was an asset in this study, I realized at the outset that it could also make for some difficulties. I had to consider what I would do if my research participants were engaging in activities which put them at risk for contracting HIV. I thought it might be difficult for me to listen to their stories without offering counseling and sex education. I had encountered this problem when I was learning to do qualitative research by interviewing young people about their feelings on teenage pregnancy. I learned that some adolescents in that study had relatives with AIDS and were sexually active, but they were not practicing safer sex.

That experience posed an ethical dilemma which forced me to reflect on the most responsible and effective way of dealing with the problem of potentially self-destructive behavior. Many of the young people with whom I came into contact chose not to accept well-intentioned and competently delivered counseling and sex education from me and other professionals. I realized that the sex education and counseling I provided, although a relief to me, were not effective when the individual was not prepared to listen. Furthermore, my attempts at providing these services could have compromised my rapport with interviewees, who may have felt judged and perhaps were inhibited from expressing their views freely. This could have impaired my attempt to gain insight into their behavior.

I still feel that this is a difficult ethical dilemma, but I believe that the problem can best be addressed by attempting to understand the behavior, rather than seeking with limited success to immediately prevent it. As a researcher my role is not to change the views of participants but to elicit and explore those views. A non-judgmental stance is necessary to give participants the freedom to say what they feel. This is essential in order to gain insight into their behavior. These insights might subsequently be used to develop intervention strategies. I believe that this is ultimately the best way to deal with this problem. Herdt and Boxer (1991) advocated the use of qualitative methodology to explore AIDS related issues in order to develop "a specialized knowledge base from which to construct experience-near, self-esteem enhancing [AIDS prevention] interventions that are meaningful to the target group" (p. 177).

I came to this study with a deep concern about AIDS. The dimensions of the epidemic may not be readily discernible to many people, especially those who are not among the currently most severely affected demographic groups, such as gay white males and poor urban people of color. However, I have found that one need only look beneath the surface to encounter it. I originally got the idea for this study through my work with a group of 9th graders on the Lower East Side in the late 1980's. I brought up the issue of AIDS one day in our counseling group and was surprised at their uncharacteristic resistance to talking. I persisted with the topic the next week with the naive belief that they didn't know much about AIDS. I was stunned when one by one, five of the eight group members then disclosed that they had family members, mostly aunts and uncles, who had AIDS. At that time the conventional wisdom in the field of AIDS prevention was that if only teenagers knew someone with AIDS they would take it seriously and abstain or practice safer sex. However, the pregnancy rate in that small junior high, where many teens were affected by AIDS, was an alarming 22%, which indicated a high level of unprotected sex and flouted the conventional wisdom. This experience, and talks with a teenager who had lost two siblings to AIDS but did not practice safer sex, are what prompted this study. My aim from the outset was not to focus on prevention issues such as safer sex because that was too narrow a lens. I wanted to learn, from the perspective of the affected adolescents, what their concerns were and how the experience of having a family member with AIDS affected them.

I initially began to explore the research question with the belief that sexuality would be a major theme for the young people. Since HIV can be transmitted sexually, I thought that the experience of having a close family member with AIDS might have a great impact on adolescents' feelings about their sexuality. Qualitative methodology, which focuses on the participants' concerns rather than those of the researcher, enabled me to branch off from this line of inquiry as other themes with equal or greater resonance for the young people emerged. By remaining open to their concerns, feelings and·ideas I was able to identify and explore areas which I hadn't anticipated at the outset of the study. I used qualitative techniques to ensure trustworthiness, such as making my reasoning public through analytic memos and peer debriefing (detailed below) to uncover and counter any biases on my part that might affect my conception, conduct and analysis of this study.

RATIONALE FOR METHOD

When I began this research the impact on young people of having a mother with AIDS had been relatively unexplored. Unfortunately, there is still a paucity of research in this area. Geballe et al., in one of the few books devoted to this topic, write that uninfected children and youth affected by AIDS in their families are "largely invisible to both the academic and service communities . . . the scholarly literature has been virtually devoid of research concerning [their] experience" (1995, p. xi). Little is known about what the concerns and special needs of adolescents and young adults are as a result of the presence of AIDS in their families and how the disease affects their feelings about themselves and their behavior. Qualitative methodology is the methodology of choice in exploring a situation in which one seeks to learn about the issues that are most pertinent to the experience of the participants.

Qualitative methodology is flexible and recursive, continually returning to the words of the participants to guide subsequent inquiry. This allowed my conceptualization of the topic to evolve as the research progressed, because it gave prominence to the input of research participants. The initial part of the study focused on learning what the important questions were for the study, and "the problem of interest [arose] from the respondent's reaction to the broad issue" (Guba & Lincoln, 1981, P. 155). The recursive nature of qualitative methodology permitted me to formulate questions as the study progressed in order to explore significant trends emerging in the ongoing interviews. This shaped the basic research question to correspond to the issues which were most important to the participants. An example of this process is how the original question, which revolved around the experience of teenagers who had family members with AIDS, evolved into an exploration of young people whose mothers had AIDS. This fine-tuned responsiveness to the data is a major asset of qualitative methodology, and it enabled me to note and develop ideas which originated from unexpected dimensions of the material, such as the intense mother-child conflict and the significance of childbearing.

Qualitative methodology allows the intensive study of a small number of participants. Data are gone over thoroughly and repeatedly to discern patterns, formulate conceptualizations and illuminate further directions for subsequent inquiry. In this way ideas emerge from the material itself, rather than from a priori hypotheses, and understanding of the research question deepens as the study progresses. The method is inductive and recursive; "abstractions are built as the particulars are grouped together" (Bogdan & Bicklen, p. 29). As a researcher I first cast a wide net and then narrowed in on significant, recurring ideas and tried to elucidate themes that tied together those ideas.

Qualitative methodology is capable of conveying substantial depth of analysis. This derives from several of its salient characteristics. First, data are collected within their natural context, so that contextual clues as to meaning are preserved. Second, the method focuses simultaneously on multiple dimensions of the question rather than isolating single aspects to be studied and controlling for extraneous variables. This yields complex, specific detail and allows the natural structure and complexity of the subject to emerge. The emphasis on data in context and the capacity to include multiple dimensions of a problem, which are central to the qualitative method, contribute to its ability to discern and convey complex and subtle phenomena.

RECRUITING PARTICIPANTS

Recruiting participants was a particularly arduous process. Because of the stigma and secrecy surrounding AIDS it was difficult to find young people whose mothers had AIDS. Even more frustrating, when I did identify possible particpants, the young people were often inaccessible. For one thing, they moved around a great deal, even during the short time I was in contact with them. Some did not have a phone in the house and relied on relatives or friends to get messages to them. Because of this lack of a stable home base and phone number, contacting them was very difficult. In addition, although they seemed eager to talk when I first explained the study, some prospective participants failed to show up for appointments. Several times I was left standing on street corners, waiting vainly for a participant to show up. Despite careful planning, at one point I was stood up six times in a row. The participants forgot, they were unreachable, or they had another commitment. When they did show up, they were often very late. I think part of the reason for this may be that AIDS is such a difficult subject to talk about, given the stigma, fear and despair attached to it.

I recruited my first potential participant from a teen theater group in a low-income urban area. We met twice to talk about the study, and she told me she had lost two uncles to AIDS and suspected her mother, a former heroin user, might have AIDS. She then participated in an interview, but she failed to show up for three separate follow-up interviews. Part of the reason for this was that she moved three times, including one eviction, in the five months during which we were in contact. When I last spoke with her she was thinking about moving again, this time with a friend's family. I was not able to include her as a participant because I had only one interview with her.

I tried recruiting from other sources, such as community based organizations and through contacts in the fields of education and social services. Although I identified several prospective participants, it was very difficult to sustain contact with them because they lacked telephones or were moving. One young woman, whose mother had died of AIDS, kept promising to come for an interview but always failed to show up. She finally told me over the phone that she was just too distraught to meet with me and feared that the stress of talking about her deceased mother would harm her unborn baby.

I asked colleagues in public schools if they knew any teenagers who might want to participate in my study. However, AIDS is classified information and is not even permitted in confidential written reports. This made it difficult for other clinicians to share information, and sometimes they themselves did not know of the presence of AIDS in the family of a counselee.

I kept networking, and through a friend I learned of a community center in a low-income area. The director, whom I call Sarah, acted as a gatekeeper and connected me with two young people she knew who were affected by AIDS.

Both of them agreed to speak with me and became participants in the study. One was a young man of 19, whom I call Joe in this study. The other was a young woman of 18, whom I call Maria.

Although I work at a school in another low-income area with a number of teenagers who are affected by AIDS in their families, I felt I could not ask any of them to participate in the study because I did not want to compromise my counseling relationship with them. The feelings and experiences they shared with me were very helpful in grounding my perception of the experiences of the participants in the study, and they often corroborated them. One young woman, with whom I'd had a very close counseling relationship continued to call me after she graduated from the school, saying that she wanted to talk. Her mother had recently died of AIDS, and I referred her to an agency for counseling. She took the referral but said she wanted to speak with me as well, because of the support I had given her in the past. I grappled with the idea of inviting her to participate in the study. I felt concern because I didn't want to foster an unrealistic dependence on me or blur the boundaries that had served us so well in our counseling relationship. However, I needed a participant, and she wanted to talk, so, with permission from my advisor, I invited her to participate in the study.

This twenty year old woman, whom I call Tina in the study, was very eager to participate and liked the idea of possibly helping other young people whose mothers were ill or had died from AIDS. She also wanted to talk about the turmoil she was experiencing following the death of her mother. I knew that she needed more than just a few interviews and occasional phone conversations with me, and at my request she agreed to begin seeing a counselor at an outside agency as well.

THE INTERVIEW PROCESS

The data for this study derive primarily from intensive interviews with my three participants, supplemented by descriptions of the contexts in which they lived. Intensive interviews may also be called ethnographic interviews (Spradley, 1979), qualitative interviews (Patton, 1980), or in-depth interviews (Lincoln & Guba, 1985). Lofland and Lofland (1984, p. 59) define the intensive interview as "a guided conversation whose goal is to elicit rich, detailed material". My goal in interviewing these young people was to be able to see the world through their eyes (Ely, 1991) in order to better understand their experience.

I interviewed participants in locations that were mutually convenient. The rooms we used were private enough to ensure that the participants would not be inhibited by the presence of others and quiet enough to permit the use of a tape recorder. These included various rooms at a community center, a seminar room at a university, and an office in a school. Prior to beginning the interviews, I told prospective participants what I was trying to accomplish in interviewing them and estimated the time commitment I would ask them to make, at least two interviews of approximately two hours each and a follow-up participant check of my findings. (See Appendix B for Statement to Participants). I explained that the interviews would be tape recorded in their entirety to preserve a record of what was said and to enable me to reflect on and analyze their exact words. I assured their anonymity and their right to review tape recordings of the interviews and take out anything they were uncomfortable with. They also had the right to withdraw at any point in the study. None of the participants chose to exercise these options. I reviewed the consent forms with them and obtained their signed consent. The three young people who actually participated in the study were 18 years of age or older and so could sign their own forms. Each of the participants received a copy of their signed consent forms.

After interviewing my first two participants I was so moved by their deprivation that I asked my advisor if I could provide participants with a stipend. I had bought both of them dinner, but I felt strongly that I wanted to give them money, both to help them in their very real struggle for survival and as a token of appreciation for contributing to the study. After receiving permission I provided participants with a stipend of $10 per interview. None of the young people were told about the stipend until after they had expressed interest in participating in the study, so It was not used as an inducement.

According to Spradley, the interviewer has two main tasks: to develop rapport and to elicit information. He defines rapport as a "basic sense of trust" which "allows for the free flow of information" (p. 78). For me, the sine qua non for establishing rapport is to view the respondents with respect, as teachers capable of revealing to me their unique experience and the meanings it has for them. Some other important aspects of establishing rapport were the language I used and my willingness to accept the respondents as they were. I encouraged them to speak in their own language, and I phrased my questions using their own words. I also tried not to convey judgment about anything they said, as this interferes with rapport and can discourage participants from responding candidly.

I began all the interviews by reviewing with participants the focus of my study (Lincoln & Guba), namely to learn about their experience as young people whose mothers either currently had AIDS or had died of the disease. Even though this had been discussed prior to the initial interview, reiterating it helped to focus both the participant and me on the task ahead. It has been my experience in interviewing teenagers that some have difficulty talking to an unfamiliar adult and may initially need some time to feel at ease. When this happened with my participants I helped them to warm up by asking a general or "grand tour" question about their lives (Spradley), such as what it was like living in their current setting. This gave them practice talking with me while "providing valuable information about how the respondent construes the general characteristics of the contexts" (Lincoln & Guba, p. 270). After that I asked them open-ended questions, such as about the nature of their relationship with their mother. I asked other questions as I followed their stories to elicit more information and to clarify points. This followed the funnel-like sequence advocated by Guba and Lincoln (1981), where the interviewer at first asks general questions and then gradually narrows the focus as the themes most relevant to the respondents become apparent and require elaboration.

I could not presuppose which dimensions would be salient for the respondents, so I had to allow them to take the lead in describing their experiences and permit them to respond in their own terms and take whatever direction they wanted. The open-ended nature of ethnographic interviews does not mean that they are unstructured (Ely, 1991). Rather, the structure of the interview was shaped by my ability to follow the thinking of my interviewees. Each participant should be "full partner in the endeavor and often provides surprising and useful directions not allowed by other, more researcher-centered interviews" (p. 58).

The importance of the role of the respondents in determining the direction of the interview did not mean that I had to be passive. I engaged in active listening, responding to their statements in order to clarify and elaborate on their meaning and to follow up on emergent ideas. The interview questions and ultimately my understanding of the problem were built on the ideas the participants expressed, and I had to be poised to note and inquire about those ideas. Since it is the respondent who defines what is important (Spradley) I needed to use a recursive approach and follow up on the participants' words, which set the course for further questions. I returned again and again to their own words, seeking greater detail and clarity. It was from this constant cycle of returning to the interviewee's own words that the design of the research emerged. I listened to participants talk about other aspects of their lives and tried to follow up on their lines of thought to learn more about what their lives were like and how they viewed things. In this way issues I had not initially considered, such as the importance of their romantic relationships and of their babies emerged.

I asked probing questions to deepen my understanding of what the participants were trying to say. This encouraged them to provide more detail, to clarify meaning or to elaborate. As the interviewer I tried to assume nothing; whenever I had a question about what they meant I used probes such as "you said . . . , tell me more," to encourage them to elaborate on their statements. I had to do this sensitively, so that they did not feel judged or harassed. One way I did this was to ask them to give me an example of what they were talking about rather than asking them what they meant. Then following Ely's recommendation, I tried to "ask and then keep still in order to listen and observe" (1991, p. 66).

Audiotaping was essential so that I could construct a verbatim transcript of each participant's words and return to the interviews and study them after the fact. Immediately after each interview I wrote field notes in my log, describing in detail my impressions of the participant and the interview experience as a whole. As soon as possible after the interview I transcribed the tape recorded data onto a computer. I included nonverbal aspects of the interaction which were in my field notes, as well as those which I recalled when I heard the recorded conversation.

I interviewed Joe and Maria twice each. I was unable to locate either one for a third, participant checking interview to sound out some of my interpretations with them to see if they made sense to them. While this loss was unanticipated and unavoidable, I was able to compensate for it because I had explored and refined my developing ideas about their first interviews with them during each of their second interviews. I interviewed Tina three times and also met for a fourth time, a participant check of my findings.

I ended the data collection phase of my study at three participants for two reasons. The first and most compelling was that it was so difficult to find participants who were willing to talk and were available over time for follow-up interviews. The instability of their housing is a major problem for many young people affected by AIDS, and it presented a great problem to me as a researcher in terms of their unavailability for a series of interviews. The second reason for stopping at three participants was that I was seeing some redundancy in the data. Certain themes, like the lack of a stable home and the way they seemed to invest their hopes for a better future in bearing children were shared and repeated by all three participants.

This qualitative study is not meant to be representative of all young people affected by the illness or death of their mother from AIDS, but rather to be a richly detailed look into what that experience is like for a few young people. Thus I stopped interviewing after three participants.

THE FIELD LOG

The field log is the written record of the research study. According to Ely, "the log is the data; only that which has been recorded there is available for research" (1991, p. 70).

My log consists of several parts. The most fundamental and voluminous are the transcriptions of the interviews with my participants. While it is a time consuming and onerous task to transcribe interviews, the process deepened my familiarity with their content. This intimacy with the participants' words helped to illuminate insights about the material.

The log also includes accounts of my feelings and reactions to the vicissitudes of the study from its inception onward. This process of "talking" to myself in the log enabled me to reflect on the study and develop my thoughts. Ely states that "the log is the place where each qualitative researcher faces the self as instrument through a personal dialogue about moments of victory and disheartenment, hunches, feelings, insights, assumptions, biases and ongoing ideas about method" (1991, p. 69).

Reflection on the descriptive and introspective content of the log creates another level, the analytic memos, which are "data about the data" (Ely, p. 70). I wrote my first analytic memo before the study began, to crystallize my thinking and feelings about the study at that time. Once I began to interview participants, my analytic memos became a means to make the ideas embedded in the data explicit. They became the first step in the analysis of the data and highlighted what needed to be done in the on-going interviews.

DATA ANALYSIS

The aim of data analysis in qualitative research is to uncover patterns existing in the data. These may be used to create themes that integrate the data (Carini, 1975, quoted in Ely, 1997).

Data analysis in qualitative research begins during the data gathering process so that it can shape the emerging direction of the study (Lincoln & Guba, 1985). The first step in my analysis of the data was to immerse myself in each of the participant's interviews in order to become as familiar with them as possible. To accomplish this I typed my field notes and the interview transcripts myself. I read and re-read the transcripts and wrote notes of my impressions and ideas in the margins. I then wrote analytic memos in my log to begin to make sense of the data. This review of the data was helpful in organizing my thinking about what the participants had told me and in noting recurring patterns or ideas. It also helped me to formulate questions for subsequent interviews so I could explore points I had missed or clarify points which were still unclear to me.

In the next level of analysis I coded the interview transcripts by hand, marking sections with terms which characterized the main idea(s) I felt were expressed or inherent in the section, such as disclosure of the mother's illness, drug use by the parent, or expressions of anger. The process of creating these categories served both to organize the data and to "tease out the meaning of [my] findings as [I] considered supporting evidence in each category and determined how categories may be linked" (Ely, 1991, p. 150). I exhausted all the data in this process, so that virtually every part of the interview was accounted for in at least one category. Some segments were coded under two or more categories. At times I found I had to expand or collapse categories to accommodate emerging patterns in the data. I also revised some of the category names, based on emerging patterns in the data. A listing of categories for each of the participants is found in Appendix C. I checked both my coding of the data and categorization with my peer support group (described below), necessitating a more public articulation of the rationale behind my choices, and I elicited and considered their reactions to my interpretations.

I then copied all the segments of the same code and pasted them together on the computer into a single document for that category. I found that combining all the segments coded under one category and reading them together increased my understanding of that idea far more than reading the segments separately.

After completing each coded document on a particular category I read it over several times, made notes in the margins and wrote an analytic memo about it. These analytic memos included specific quotes from the transcript as examples to support my impressions of the data. I also wrote some extended analytic memos, linking together several related categories.

From this point I began to create narratives for my participants. These narratives were originally arranged, not by the sequence of the interviews, but by the sequences I had created in my analytic memos. I edited for clarity and rearranged segments again for continuity, but I tried to preserve the unique voices of my participants by working from the quotes I had put together in the analytic memos.

As I shaped the narratives I continually re-read them and, using the ideas in my analytic memos, I began to write participant themes. These themes, expressed as "I" statements, epitomized what I felt to be the most salient characteristics of the participants' stories. I then fleshed out each theme, supporting it with the data from the interviews. After writing individual themes for each participant I studied these to extract what I felt were common themes for all the participants.

TRUSTWORTHINESS

The point of qualitative research is to capture the experience of those being studied in context and in as much depth and complexity as possible. Qualitative researchers have developed techniques to safeguard the integrity of their work so that, in Ely's words, "the process is carried out fairly and the findings represent as closely as possible the experience of the people who are being studied" (1991, p. 93). This quality control is called trustworthiness. The techniques I used to strive for trustworthiness included making my reasoning public, peer debriefing, and participant checking.

It is important to make one's reasoning both explicit and public when giving the rationale for any interpretive work, such as coding, categories and themes. I did this through analytic memos, peer debriefing (see below), and explanations in the dissertation itself. Not only the logical reasoning has to be made clear, but my personal biases and feelings that contribute to my judgments were also documented.

Peer debriefing is the "process of exposing oneself to a . . . peer in a manner paralleling an analytic session and for the purpose of exploring aspects of the situation that might otherwise remain only implicit in the investigator's mind" (Lincoln & Guba, p. 308). Throughout the course of data analysis I have used my support group as a check for trustworthiness. We read each other's work and candidly discussed both the reasoning processes and the emotional factors which influenced our work. This process helped to keep us "honest" as "biases are probed, meanings explored, the basis for interpretations clarified" (Ibid.). Within our group we checked working hypotheses, developed and tested next steps in the emergent design and processed feelings that might have clouded good judgment.

My peer support group gave me feedback on my initial coding of parts of interview transcripts, the process and product of the coded documents, the participant narratives and the participants' themes. Their input has enabled me to get other perspectives on the data and to guard against specious interpretations.

Participant checking (Lincoln & Guba) entails sharing selected findings with the participants in order to see how they respond to the sense I made of their experiences. This is an important test of the credibility of the study. Unfortunately I was unable to meet with two of my participants for this process. I did meet with the third to share selected findings and to get her reactions. I used her feedback to refine my preliminary analysis, always with the awareness that I am ultimately the person responsible for what is finally shared in the study.

CREATING THE PARTICIPANTS' STORIES

As teenagers and as members of minority groups, the participants in my study spoke in their own idiom. I found their words and speech rhythms expressive and even at times poetic, and I wanted to present them in as natural a form as possible to enrich my readers' experience. I therefore had to confront the question of how I could make their narratives accessible to readers who might not be familiar with their characteristic expressions, while still preserving the texture and color of their vernacular. Although I had to edit the interviews extensively in crafting them into narratives, I tried to balance the preservation of the individuals' self expression with the task of communicating their thoughts and feelings to others not familiar with their speech.

Atkinson (1992) addresses the question of the tension between the readability of ethnographic writing and its faithfulness to the experience the researcher is trying to convey. The decision of how to present the participants' speech is not just a technical or methodological one. It has moral consequences, since it determines how participants are viewed and understood by readers. I don't want to misrepresent my respondents as middle class adolescents. I want my readers to enter a world which the young people have shared with me, a world that is probably different from the readers' own and possibly outside their current experience. The way into this world is through the voices of the young people.

While I wanted to convey the participants' distinct voices, I did not want to denigrate them through overuse of unconventional spellings and thereby fall into what Preston referred to as the "Li'l Abner Syndrome" (Atkinson, p. 28). This is a decision I made while transcribing the interviews from audiotape. Thus, conventional orthography predominates in the participants' stories. However, I did preserve some colloquialisms and nonstandard English grammatical usages, which reflect the linguistic heritage of the Nuyorican (New York Puerto Rican) and African-American communities of which these young people are a part. I feel that these are valid and expressive linguistic forms, and not "incorrect" English. I hope that my decision will not diminish the dignity of the participants in the eyes of some readers or detract from their ability to empathize with the young people.

Sometimes the participants' colloquialisms convey valuable information about them, beyond their cultural and generational affiliations. For example, the expletive, "Dag" in Joe's story is a polite way of saying "damn". This expression communicates not only Joe's subculture affiliation as a minority teenager but also his frustration and his choice to modulate that frustration as a reflection of his concern for politeness and manners.

In a poem I wrote about Maria I used several words which are commonly used by many teenagers to refer to the accoutrements of marijuana smoking. However, in recognition of the fact that these words may be unfamiliar to some people, I have provided notes to this poem. I considered changing the words, but this detracted significantly from the feeling tone of the poem.

Some of the other choices I made in writing this study involve the use of literary forms not commonly found in scholarly writing. These will undoubtably jump out at readers not familiar with recent qualitative writing and may provoke questions about artificiality or arbitrariness of form. However, the current conventions prevalent in most contemporary scholarly writing are also themselves literary forms, the only difference being that they are so common as to render them invisible to the reader unused to other forms of presentation. My choice of several uncommon forms of presentation of my research, including free verse and pastiche for my participants' stories and poetry and vignette for conveying a sense of character and place, is neither arbitrary nor capricious.

Each of these rhetorical devices have qualities which particularly suit the data and enabled me to convey meaning through the form itself.

Patai (1988, p. 147) remarked on "a distance separating the spoken word from the written word that is insurmountable." I felt this comment was particularly apt, given my interview data. She advocated the use of free verse to preserve the poetic and dramatic features of an interviewee's speech. I made the decision to present some passages of the participants' stories in this way in order to capture the natural rhythms and inflections of the young people's speech and to highlight words which were accented vocally and nonverbally. Thus I was able to transpose the paralinguistic cues through the conventions of free verse, such as pauses between lines and the setting off of words for emphasis. Although this may strike some as unnatural, I find that, on the contrary, it communicates the participants' manner of speaking more clearly than conventional narrative. It is much like the process of cutting and polishing a gemstone in order to enable the structure and beauty inherent in the material to shine through. The segments of free verse are embedded in the participants' stories. I did not set them apart, as I did not want to break the narrative flow. They are not discrete poems but simply a continuation of the participants' stories in their own voices.

Another literary form which I used in presenting the participants' stories was pastiche. This technique of juxtaposing various pieces of data on the same topic creates meaning that is greater than the sum of the parts through contrast, complementarity, and amplification. Pastiche can give a "dynamic quality and a sense of immediacy as the separate pieces deliver new meaning, at times complementary and at others contradictory" (Ely, 1997, p. 100). Pastiche usually includes information from multiple sources, but I have concentrated on the participants' own words, except for two instances when I supplemented them with my own observations. All of the segments of both Joe's and Maria's pastiches are crafted from their own words, but I added my own observations in two instances in Tina's pastiches and indicated this at the end of the segments. I took this editorial license to flesh out Tina's words with my own contributions, based on my field notes and counseling notes.

I created pastiches for each of the participants, to compare and contrast disparate aspects of their thoughts, feelings and experiences on a given topic. By juxtaposing their sometimes contradictory sentiments on the same theme I was able to emphasize each opposing aspect and recreate on the page the ambivalence they conveyed. Pastiche enabled me to unify conflicting statements without artificially smoothing them over, which would have falsely represented the participant's more complex feelings. In cases where there was little contrast, the amplification of a point in different ways created a synergistic effect that added power to the ideas expressed.

I wrote both poetry and a vignette to convey a sense of the context in which my participants lived. Ely (1997, p. 135) speaks of the "intensity and compression of poetry [which] emphasizes the vividness of the moment." I used my poem, "Death on a South Bronx Sidewalk", to set the stage for the context in which all three of my participants lived, as well as to foreshadow the themes of substance abuse and despair. Similarly, the vignette of the self help group at the Center is meant to convey both a sense of the place where two of my participants lived and the theme of substance abuse. Other poems about Maria and Tina highlight themes which relate to the stories of these two young women, especially around the significance of childbearing. I indicated my authorship after each of the three poems I wrote to distinguish them from the free verse, which is composed primarily of the participants' own words.

Although the sequence of the participants' stories flows for the most part along temporal and/or thematic lines, at times the stories do not follow a sequential order in time. This is because the participants themselves moved readily between the past and present, and less often, the future. I sometimes chose to reflect this temporal fluidity in my presentation of their stories. This enabled me to preserve important clues to meaning. If I had ironed out all the material into a linear narrative, it might have obscured important relationships. The most significant example is the link between the deaths of their mothers and fathers for both Maria and Tina. For both young women, discussing their mother's deaths immediately and repeatedly brought to the surface the older and still unresolved grief at their father's death.

CHAPTER IV

The Young People's Stories

INTRODUCTION

The results of this study consist of the stories of the three young people who participated, as well as material pertaining to the neighborhoods in which they lived. This section begins with a brief overview of some of the social and economic characteristics of their neighborhoods, as described in the literature, and a poem that presents an important aspect of the social and emotional landscape there. This is followed by a more specific description of the Center in which two of the participants lived and a vignette of a meeting of recovering drug addicts held there. The participants' stories follow. Each one is preceded by an introduction and followed by an analysis of the main themes which were distilled from the stories.

Much of the analysis of the stories is spread throughout this chapter, interspersed with the stories. Only the common themes, which cut across participants, are found in a separate section.

SETTING

The young people I interviewed for this study came from New York City's Lower East Side and the South Bronx, two low-income urban areas whose populations consisted mainly of African-Americans and people of Puerto Rican descent. Both of these neighborhoods have gained notoriety because of their endemic poverty, crumbling infrastructure, and severe drug abuse problems. When the participants in my study were young children, their neighborhoods were rapidly undergoing destructive changes. Fitzpatrick (1990, p. 109) referred to the "burning of the Bronx" in the mid 1970's, when two South Bronx census tracts lost 57% of all residential units. Wallace (1988, p. 2) described the "loss of housing and destruction of community" in both the Lower East Side and the South Bronx during the mid 1970's.

The physical destruction of the infrastructure in these two communities was mirrored by the devastation of lives wrought by poverty, racism, family disintegration, and drug use, especially heroin. Both were hit hard by an epidemic of heroin use in the 1960's and 70's (National Research Council, 1993). The photojournalist Biddle (1992) documented the effects of poverty and heroin use on the Lower East Side in the late 1970's and again in the late 1980's, taking photographs of residents and recording their thoughts about the pictures. Violence and heroin use were commonplace in both decades. In the late 80's the ravages of AIDS were familiar to intravenous drug users and their families, but because of the stigma of AIDS, victims and their loved ones in Biddle's book often denied they had the disease.

"The geography of drug abuse ... is largely the geography of AIDS." (Wallace, p. 12) Heroin has been endemic for decades in these two neighborhoods. Not surprisingly, they have some of the highest rates of AIDS infection in the country. The overall adult incidence of AIDS for the South Bronx in 1997 was 2628 per 100,000. (New York City Department of Health [NYCDOH], April, 1997 p. 12) Similarly, on the Lower East Side, the incidence was 2540 cases per 100,000. (Ibid.) Although women make up only 21% of reported AIDS cases in the city (Ibid., p. 10), their relative numbers are increasing. The death rate for American women continues to increase, even while the overall AIDS death rate is dropping (CDC, 1997a). Of particular relevance to this study is the rate of AIDS infection for women of color. African-American women make up 53% and Latinas 34% of all cases of AIDS in women in the city (NYCDOH, April, 1997, p. 4).

Wallace's term, the "synergism of plagues" referred to the mathematical model he used to track the interrelated progression of drug abuse, housing loss, poverty, and AIDS. It is equally apt to describe the psychological impact of these and other social ills on the residents of the two communities. The interaction of poverty, racism, violence, drug abuse, and AIDS can compromise an individual's ability to cope with each separate factor, so that their impact together is far more devastating than just their combined effects. Often AIDS is just one more insurmountable problem in a life filled with grievous adversity. As such, it may not even be perceived as the most compelling issue confronting the person.

I have worked in both neighborhoods, starting on the Lower East Side as a teacher from 1979 to 1983 and again, as a psychologist-in-training from 1988 to 1992. I have been working as a school psychologist in the South Bronx since the spring of 1992. A scene I encountered walking near my school with several neighborhood teenagers inspired the following poem, which I feel captures an important aspect of the physical and emotional landscape of both neighborhoods.

Death on a South Bronx Sidewalk

The dog lay like a filthy, tattered grey rug,
Almost inert on the sidewalk.
Rumpled, as though it had been
Kicked into a pile by passersby,
With wrinkles of ribs so sharp
They almost pierced the decrepit hide.
It heaved feebly, almost imperceptibly,
Its open mouth receiving precious little air,
Instead expiring life
On to the oblivious cement.
An eye, or was it just a socket,
Meat-red and sunken,
Blind to all without
Looked inward in a vain search for life.
There was no hope.
The body had been ground so low
The spirit could no longer abide.
Death was already wresting it out of its
Mangy prison of skin and bone.
Not five feet away sat three men and a woman,
Motionless, bottles in hand.
They stared blankly, nursing a noon time high that would
Descend with the sun to total stupefaction by night,
Keeping unseeing watch over the desperate spectacle
Of their deepest fears:
Abandonment, suffering, decay,
And worst of all
The awful inevitability that bound the lives on this sidewalk.
They took long draughts out of the bottles,
Whose sinister contents lurked beneath brown paper bags,
Seeking perhaps to wash life back down their throats,
But instead forcing it out through their every pore.
Blank. Numb.
This was death.
This was life,
Seeping out on to the indifferent sidewalk.

This poem reflects an environment where it is unremarkable to see suffering and people numbed and incapacitated by substance abuse. Although the circumstances are desperate, for the people in the poem despair is not anguished or urgent. It is muted by substance abuse, but it persists, chronic and pervasive. This is a significant feature of the environment in which the participants in this study live.

The Center

"The Center" is a half-way house for recovering addicts, run by Sarah, a free spirited, fiercely independent, 60's style activist. Sarah proudly told me that more than a hundred meetings of Alcoholics Anonymous and Narcotics Anonymous were held every week in the two cavernous four story buildings that make up the Center. The Center also sheltered twenty or so teenagers from chemically dependent families. Many of these teens had mothers and fathers with AIDS. Sarah had been taken to court for being unlicensed, and her funding sources were uncertain at best. She was recommended to me by an administrator in a neighborhood school, who felt she provided a home for teenagers who had nowhere else to go.

When I first spoke with Sarah on the phone she was receptive to my study. She said that I could come and speak to the young people about it; as long as I brought pizzas I would be welcome. The afternoon of my visit I called to confirm, and Sarah apologized for being "lax". She said that she didn't think the kids would be back because she hadn't played up the fact that I was coming. She also told me that she had been having problems for insisting that the teenagers not use or sell drugs, and they were rebelling. She complained about the difficulty of getting understanding of their problems and getting funding for services for them. She launched into a lengthy tirade against the "politically correct" gay activists whom she felt controlled AIDS services, stating that for the most part they don't know about parenting teens. I told her that I hoped to explore and call attention to the plight of these young people. She said she realized that, but had a lot to get off her chest.

Sarah suggested that I attend a Narcotics Anonymous meeting at the Center to better understand the problem of substance abuse, which she saw as the root of many of the other problems of the neighborhood. Sarah told me she did not run the meetings; they were run by the participants themselves, but she provided space for the many groups which met at the Center. I went to a morning meeting later that week. It was intense, but also very informal. The room was crowded with people, most of whom sat on white plastic chairs facing an old grey desk at the front of the room. A few additional chairs were arrayed facing the side of the desk. At the desk a woman of about 35 talked about her days of "drugging" and all the degrading acts she had committed to get money for drugs. Most people were attentive and offered occasional supportive comments, such as "Yeah!"

Most of the approximately sixty people in the room were African-American or Latino. Most were men, with about fifteen women and several small children, who walked about the room. Every so often someone walked quietly to the back to drink coffee from a large urn or talk privately with another participant. Some people left, and more came in. Many of the people wore old clothes, but a few were dressed fashionably, including one woman in a green velvet outfit with a matching hat. One man slept on the floor throughout the entire meeting, while near him a woman, who seemed to be agitated and unfocused, looked haphazardly through a plastic bag and occasionally paced.

As the meeting went on other people spoke about their lives with and without drugs. One young man was particularly graphic and moving, talking about how he once lost bodily control and defecated in his pants in excitement when he had managed to get enough money to buy more drugs. Another speaker advised that people be tested for AIDS and that they bring another recovering addict with them for support. Two other speakers spoke out against what they felt was sexual manipulation of neophytes in the program by more advanced community members.

I felt that most people there were telling of their experiences as they had lived them, exorcising the degradation brought on them by drugs. Their stories were stinging, bracing, like the cold, snowy air outside. I felt solemn and touched. When the meeting ended the participants formed a circle with arms around each other. A young black man looked surprised when I approached him to join the circle as it was forming, but he accepted me and put his arm around me. Most people recited the twelve step prayer: "Lord, grant me the serenity to accept what I cannot change, the courage to change what I can, and the wisdom to know the difference." I headed out into the snowy day thinking how important telling one's story is in healing.

JOE

After several long telephone conversations, I was looking forward to finally meeting Sarah in person and to meeting my first participant. I arrived on the block where the Center was located. It was raucous, dirty and hip, crowded with teenagers in punk garb and older, tired and unkempt looking adults in hip clothing. The buildings Sarah's program were housed in had been the site of various popular dance clubs from the 1960's through the 1980's. On the afternoon of my visit its long stoops were crowded with people, most seeming to be in their twenties through forties, and many with the hard look of junkies. Passing through the throng I noticed a heavy woman with a long hippie-like dress. She stood out because she wore a clerical collar. It caught my eye, and I was surprised to see long hair and eye make-up above it. I smiled to myself in appreciation of what I thought was her fashion statement for a Friday night on the avenue.

I went upstairs to the unwelcoming second floor. A young man at the desk told me that Sarah wasn't there. However, as I was talking to him someone called, "Miss Duncan?" I turned toward an alcove I hadn't noticed at first. It was very dark, except for the glow of a television on several people sitting on old couches watching it. A thin teenage boy with baggy jeans was calling me. He held a skillet in one hand and a fork in the other and was hungrily shoveling a mixture of rice and corn from the skillet into his mouth as he spoke to me. He told me his name and that he would talk to me, as Sarah had an errand to do. He handed the skillet to another young man in the alcove who ate out of it with the same fork "Joe" had used.

Joe brought me down to a big room on the first floor. We took two of the white plastic chairs from the stacks against the wall and sat down. I looked for one that wasn't dirty, but there were no clean ones. As I sat down I noticed the arm on mine was broken. The others didn't look much better, so I tried to make myself comfortable.

Joe was small and thin, with a sallow olive complexion. He had a narrow moustache and wavy black hair. His ears were very small and slightly irregular. One of them was crumpled, like a carnation. When he talked he was direct and composed. However, whenever he moved his hands I noticed how they trembled, making him appear fragile and vulnerable. He coughed frequently, but in spite of this he smoked two cigarettes, asking my permission before he lit up the first one.

A few people passed through the room as we talked. Most greeted Joe, and one asked how the baby was. The woman with the clerical collar came in, and to my surprise I found out that this was Sarah. Joe was both affectionate and distant from her. He greeted her with warm words but became remote when she worried about his plans for the evening, a visit to a distant skating rink. When Sarah left Joe resumed his story.

When I returned for a second interview three weeks later, Joe seemed perturbed. We left the Center to find a restaurant, as I had promised to buy him dinner. He walked quickly and without looking at me. He did look long at two attractive teenage girls on the street, stopping dramatically and turning to look after them when they passed us. When I commented on it he seemed pleased and relaxed somewhat. He said he was thinking of moving back to the Center because it was getting too expensive living with his mother. He said that out of his $300 Supplemental Security Income check he had to pay her $275. He thought his mother should move too, back into a hotel. He said that she was probably going to die soon, and that he would go to the funeral but wouldn't cry, because that would bring up too much pain.

Joe told me he would get no rest at home because his baby daughter would be crying. He was going to call the baby's mother and tell her to come and get her. He told me he would tell the baby's mother that he would see the baby when he wanted to, but not to drop her off with him. His mother was caring for the baby, but since he described his mother's behavior as "bugging", it didn't sound like a very good arrangement. He said he didn't want to talk next week, and it would be better if we waited a longer time. As he crossed the main street and disappeared into the crowd I was struck by how recklessly he walked in front of oncoming cars, disregarding the obvious danger.

Joe's Story

When I was small I used to live with my mother, but I don't remember that. I was about seven when the building we were living in caught fire or something, so my mother had to move. They put us in a shelter, and they found us an apartment. That's when we moved to the projects. But then, when I was about eight,
I had to go live in a group home
Cause my mother
Couldn't take care of me
So I had to
I was there a couple of months
I was
Troubled
I couldn't sit in my seat and stuff
I don't really like
To talk about it
Cause it doesn't do
Nothing
Talking about how
Your parents
Didn't stick
How they weren't
There for you
It bothers me

From there my mother took me up again, and I started living with her. I was better off. I used to go to school, go outside, then go home and watch cartoons. We had cable, big color tv, big living room. This guy, he helped her get the apartment. Then, they had to go to Puerto Rico. She left me in the house with some people I didn't know, and they robbed us. They stole our stuff. I couldn't do nothing about it. I had went out to school, and I came back and our stuff was gone. I was about ten.

My mother always did drugs. Her and her boyfriend had a little criminal problem, selling drugs, and she got caught up, and they sent her to jail when I was like, eleven. Before she got locked up, I was staying over my aunt's. I was just visiting on the weekends. Something like that. That's when they called up.
Joe
Your mother's in jail
I was surprised
I was a little kid
It hurt
But it doesn't hurt
Any more

When my mother first got locked up I stayed with my aunt for a little while. But my aunt didn't like me for some reason. So I felt like being bad with her. She put me out of the house for something I did. It's personal. I don't like to tell about it. So then I left, and I never came back.
In a way
My mother ruined my life
She made it hard for me
Real hard
I was going from house to house
Because she went to jail
So much problems came to us
Cause of her going to jail
I lived in people's houses
I didn't really like
They used to beat me
And didn't treat me right
For no reason

From my aunt's house I went to this lady Milagros' house. That's that lady who used to beat me. Her daughter used to always be like, "You better stop hitting him. You know you gonna get in trouble." Milagros was really fucked up. She didn't care. She was fucking with drugs. She always used to be laying in bed, talking shit. I used to just mind my business and watch cartoons. Try to keep on the down low. Stay out of her way.

I was with her a couple of months. Something like that. I wasn't living so well. I was skinny and so puny. She was beating on me so much that my mother found out. My mother was in jail, but she called up this lady, Gladys. She asked her, "Can you do me a favor? Can you take my son out of where he's at?" And I left to Gladys, and then from there it got better. I stayed with her for five years, and she took care of me. She bought me clothes. From there I started living a little better.

When I lived with Gladys
I learned a lot of things
I learned how to take care of myself
She's not my real aunt
But she took care of me like it
I had my own job all the time
I always used to go to school
I used to pass my grades
Put it like this
Dag man!
I was good when I was in 6th to 9th grade
I did everything
As good as possible

After my mother had went to jail, that's when she found out she had AIDS. I think she got it because she was shooting up. I think that's what it was. I don't really know. I wasn't with the details. I didn't really know until the time it started getting serious. She started talking to me about it when she was inside the jail. She was letting me know, I'm sick, sick. But I didn't really know, until she came out. That's when she told me. She didn't want to tell me.

After my mother did the bit, she came out of jail, and I started living with her again. I was in 10th grade. When my mother came out of jail, that's when I really fucked up. I was switched. Like, I couldn't think. Know what I'm saying? I was like Dag! This, this, that, that. I knew that she was sick. But I was like, what can I do? I can't do nothing about it. If she dies, she dies. If she lives, she lives. I can't do nothing. I gotta live on with my life also.

Let me see
How can I put it
(Sigh)
It was like
In ways I think about
Tomorrow
All the time
The future
You know
Get to the next day
Cause the next day's gonna be
A different day
And then
Get to the next day

Again

Cause it's gonna be

A different day

When she came out of jail a lot of problems occurred. Because she was
living with this lady, and the lady, she was gay. So that, messed up my head.
Then I started noticing things change. She started taking drugs again. Smoking
crack. And the crack started messing her up. She started selling drugs. And then
from there stuff got crazy. I started selling drugs, and I dropped out of school.

Around that time, me and my mother would argue a lot. So I'd be like,
alright, whatever, I'm out. I'd leave the house and just break out. I went to chill
and hang out. This kid I was chilling with introduced me to the Center, and I
started hanging there.

I started talking about my problems in meetings at the Center. We had our own group, Addicted Teens Anonymous, with our own 12 steps. We're just like NA and AA. Help each other out. If there's a problem we sit down and try to solve it.

There's a lot of kids
Out there
That come from
Chemical dependent
Families
Like me
They're going through
The same
Problems
And the only alternative
Is go out there and
Get high
It's what they're gonna do
They'll hang out
On the corner
Where it's drug infested
Or they'll drink 40's
Just get high

I quit selling drugs, and I moved in to the Center. Sarah treated me good. But I used to fuck up. We used to fight and do a lot of crazy things. One day I took Sarah's clippers. Me and this kid robbed the store right across the street. He cut the gate! I just gave him the clippers and he gave me some of the merchandise. I sold it somewhere. They never found out. Sarah found out.
Sarah: You did wrong.
Joe: I'll make it up.
Sarah: No matter what, you gonna have to work it out. I could throw you out. You know that.
Joe: Dag! I got a choice, to go out in the street, or stay with Sarah.
I kept with her.

JOE
THE CENTER

I go through so much
Stress
When I come to the
Drug Free Disco
At the Center
I get off
Cause like
This is my tick off
Know what I'm saying
When I come over here
And they put music
On the dance floor
A lot of people come
Me and my brother
Edwin
We watch
Everybody into the
Hip, hip, hip-hop
Hip, hip-hop
We just get excited!
Just want to dance!
And I be rocking
And stuff like that
Me and him are
Dance partners
We consider each other
Brothers
So we dance
And me and my brother
Could dance good!
We did a show for the
New York Times
We got paid for that
It was a really good thing

WE WERE THE KIDS FROM
THE CLUB
BLACK POLKA DOT SHIRTS
BLOND HAIR
ME TOO
I HAD BLOND TIPS
EVERYBODY USED TO ALWAYS
KNOW US

When I moved to the Center, I shared a room with Edwin. Then from there, I asked for a room. I was doing good. Sarah said, alright, cool and gave me my own room.

SARAH ALWAYS LIKED ME, NO MATTER WHAT, SHE ALWAYS CARED FOR ME. CAUSE OUTA ALL OF THE KIDS, I WAS ONE OF THE GOODEST ONES. THEY CALL ME GOODY.

At the beginning the other kids treated me bad cause they wanted to see if I'd fight back. I used to hit them back. They used to tell me, "Yo, come on, we're all gonna go up in the attic and slap box."
Every time when we get together, it was funny. We had our own little UN. We was bugging around and shit. We was fighting and bugging out, screaming, yelling aahhh! Throwing shit all over the place. Really dirtied up the house, man. We were having fun! Yeah, it was like this. There wasn't nothing to do, there was gonna be something to be doing. Know what I'm saying? Just to do it.

If it wasn't for Sarah, this place would not be open. The self help Center, the Club for the kids. A lot of teenagers been coming here a lot. It's cool at the Club. It's better when there's more kids. I used to like it, cause we used to have the whole crew. That was when we was all living there. We would share things with each other. I was living there for three years, and I got to know everybody real good. It was like my own playground. I didn't have to go anywhere to have fun. They were living in the house. We would hang out, play basketball, go to our room and stuff like that. It was fun.

Sarah could relate to us. Because we were teenagers having a little fun. Sometimes she would get mad. I would admit what I did. See, you argue with her, she'll argue with you all night long. So I would be like, "Uh Sarah, sorry. May I be excused?" Cause she gonna keep on. She'll bring up the past, things that you did wrong. I used to do bad things, but she always considered me one of the goodest ones.

I consider myself Goody
I started that
And everybody Goody
Goody
Goody
Goody this
Goody that
Everybody started calling
Me
I felt good
Cause
At least
Damn
At least I found
A thing
You know what I'm saying?

Sarah never really did anything for me. She never really bought me nothing. I had to buy my own clothes and stuff. She bought me food, you could say. She gave me a room. But like, money and stuff like that, I had to get that on my own. I didn't have to go out there and sell drugs. I get a check from my Social Security. She looked out for me in ways. But sometimes I really wanted something I didn't have, and she wouldn't give it to me, she would give it to the girls. She used to buy them clothes and stuff. She used to always give to them. I used to get mad at her. Damn! I wished I could get stuff from her. I tried that. She said get your own money.

Sarah introduced me to this school, and they helped me out. It's hard for me because I go through so much problems, but now I go to school, like from nine o'clock to one, and I go to work from one 'til four. They got me a job working in a hospital. It's hectic, but it's good. Keeps you out of trouble. I enjoy it so far. I just want to get paid. It's not paying yet.

Lately I've been really low, cause I been messing up, like with homework and stuff. But I'm trying to bring work to school everyday. See, they hit me off with a lot of work. And I understand it, I'll bring it in. That's all I have to do. I only got 25 credits. I need 15 more to pass, and plus, the Regents Competency Tests. And those tests ain't gonna be so easy. So, it could be maybe a 50%

chance that I'll graduate. (voice very strained here) I'm trying to get there. It's hard. But, I'm trying you know. Basically, now I'm trying to deal with my life. I'm trying not to let everything stress me.

I have a permanent disability. They always said I was disabled. It's hard for me to learn things. I try my best to learn. I told my principal that I need a tutor. She said in two weeks. So I'm like, I had told her a long time ago and she told me two weeks. Another two weeks? I thought, Oh, God! If I was to get a tutor, it would help me out. I need a tutor to sit down with me and explain to me what to do and how to do it. Just, step by step. Cause I learn even more better like that. Once I know how to do it like that, I can get my math, my reading. I know how to read. That's the good thing about it. But there's some words I might not really understand. Some work is hard and some work is easy. Math is a little hard.

I got this homework
It was about a Puerto Rican guy
He comes to talk to these kids
About staying in school
And stuff like that
It was hard for him
He used to mess around
Like me
That kind of
Touched me
Cause I was like
Dag!
All this stuff that
He went through
And still
He made it
If he can do it
I can do it too
But
He's more different
From me
That's just a piece of paper
Saying something
It could be a lie
It could be truth

When I was young
Lots of girls used to
Diss me
I used to get mad
Be feeling lonely
No girls and
Stuff like that
Dag, man!
I'm a bad person
I don't get
No girls at all?
You know
What I'm saying?
But now I get girls.
After I started living at
The Center
I got plenty of
Girlfriends.
Plenty
You know it

Me and Edwin, we would call ourselves the macks. We used to get mad girls. Edwin used to always be like, "Yo, Good, I got two girls." And I always would push the move. I used to find girls, and I used to hook him up, and he used to find girls and hook me up. I used to hook him up more than what he'll hook me up with. Understand? I love that shit. **I LOVE GIRLS!**

Everyone used to come dancing with girls. We had girls who used to come see us, our own girls. The girls at the Club used to rat on us, cause we used to have our girls upstairs. Sarah used to let us be in the living room, but not in our rooms. Only thing she don't want, is for some-body there will pop up pregnant. So we would pretend like we were going out. I'd lie to Sarah, then I'd tell the guys, "Yo, do this

JOE
GIRLS & SEX

and do that. I'm gonna stuff in the room and chill with a girl." Then I'd jump all up in her skin.

I got in trouble with Sarah cause my girlfriend Gloria got pregnant. That's when I left the Center. Sarah was like, "No matter what, you're always welcome to stay." But Gloria ruined it. Because, we had lied to Sarah. I told Sarah that Gloria was 18, and she looked 18, so Sarah believed it. Meanwhile, she was only 15. Sarah got mad. I was telling Gloria "Yo, don't say nothing." And she fucked up my whole shit. Because, there could have been a problem. It could have been bad for the Center. They had problems in the past. There used to be bad things said. Like, young girls go there and get molested, or something like that.

Every second of
Every day
Every moment
Somebody's dying
Somebody just had
A baby girl
Or a baby boy
People are having
Sex
Right now
All over
Everybody does it
People gotta
Think about it
Me
I'm gonna stop
Fucking around
I'm gonna get busy

With condoms
I'm not trying to
Get no disease!

I caught one little, major disease. Crabs! From this girl. That shit got me mad! I was like damn. I never had that. I told her, "Don't ever talk to me." She knew. She just played herself. Didn't tell me. Sitting like a sucker, thinking, "Damn!" Next thing you know, something's wrong with me. I was gonna kill the girl.

I think about AIDS
Because
My mother has it
I'm scared
That's the life threat
Right there
You don't have to do
Nothing bad
Just have some fun
Having sex and all that
Without a condom
And there you go
You get it
That's it
Hopefully
I will not
(strangling voice)
Trying not to
(voice still strangled)
Cause I did things with
Girls
Without a condom

I already talked to Sarah about coming back. I can't take it with my mother bugging. She said, "You always have a place here. Only thing is, you come back, you can't be chasing after every girl you see, like last time." I'm gonna get mine anyway. You know what I'm saying. If I live there or not. No matter what, I'm gonna do mines. But I ain't gonna try to fuck up.

I didn't use condoms when I was in love with Gloria. She had my kid. The baby's gonna be a month old tomorrow. Gloria messed up. She used to get high a lot. She's a blunthead. She smokes too much weed. Tell her not to do something and she does it. She fucked a kid that I don't like, before she was pregnant.

Joe: Yo, if you did what you did, just leave me alone. If you did it, break out.
Gloria: It's over with him. I love you. I care about you. You're the only person I want to be with right now.
Joe: Yo, It's over. I'm tired of all these little games.
Gloria: But Goody, I'm pregnant with your kid. I want to be with you.
Joe: Yo, you're violating me. You fucked with me, I'm going to make you feel fucking stupid.
Gloria: What do you mean?
Joe: I fucked Lissette. I did that cause of what you did to me.
Gloria: How could you do it with Lissette? She's my best friend.
Joe: It's over, I don't want to be with you no more. You get me sick.

So she started messing around when she was pregnant. I was like, Yo, man. How you gonna do that? At least if you wanted to have sex, you could've had it with me. Cause that's my baby. Or if not, you could've just waited. But no. She wanted to do this, and do that. And always getting high. I regret her for a lot of things that she did. She played herself on me. After I found out I said,
Dag man!
I cared about her
I even cried for this girl
Know what I'm saying?
I loved her
Cause she was so nice to me
And she was fly
She had it going on!
Everywhere I would go with her
Guys would look at her
I still love her and
I care about her
She was my sweetheart
She looked out for me
And I looked out for her
But
She played herself
She started doing things

With other people
That I knew
It was like
She did such and such
With this one
And I found out
Dag!
That's fucked up
And then she did such and such
With another person
And such and such
With another person
I was like
At least
If you're gonna do something
With somebody else
Please do me a favor and
Use a condom
I heard that she didn't
But
You know
As time flew
And stuff like that
I didn't catch nothing
She didn't catch nothing
So
You know

It was by mistake I got her pregnant. At first, I was like, "Get an abortion." But then, things started flying by. I was like, "Dag, get an abortion," but then I was like, "Look, I'm taking my responsibility. The only thing I don't want you to do, is don't try to play me with your kid. I want it to get my last name." That's what I did. I signed the papers. I wasn't there when she gave birth, but she called me and she was like, "Yo, I had a baby girl."

After the baby was born she was like, "You make my life miserable. I make yours miserable." She gets me mad. I feel like yoking her, like grabbing her. She does things that I don't like and I'm like, "Yo, man, if you gonna go do it, then just leave me alone." Next thing, she comes back. And she starts talking mad and I'm like, "Yo, you just shut up!" She likes to argue about all the little things I'm not doing.

Shut up
Don't say nothing

Avoid the problem
I feel like not arguing with you
Get the point?
Just leave me alone
    She knew that was over. I still see her and the baby and stuff. I can see her
whenever I want. I don't see her all the time, cause I don't have a lot of time.
A lot of people see my daughter
And say
She's gorgeous
She's beautiful
And it feels good!
I certainly have to
Cherish that
Cause I got something now
To live for
And I hope I will never have to
Go do anything
Bad
To make money out there
Before
When I was dealing drugs
I had wads of
Money
Know what I'm saying?
Cause it's hard
So far
It's alright
I do as best as I can

This one friend that I know, his father used to come to the Center, and his father died from AIDS. When I found out, it was like, "Damn, man. I'm sorry. Take care of yourself." You know what I'm saying?

Cause it hurts. It hurts. And, it's hard for me, cause, I really don't know what I would do if my mom dies. Don't know. Probably come back here to the Center. Just live with Sarah. I'd just try to do my best.

I don't talk too much
About my mother
Because, it's hard
The bad thing about it is
You can't do
Nothing
About it
It's already happened
You can't do
Nothing
But then it's easy
What makes it easy is
When a person asks
How you feel?
How you doing?
May I help you?
Or you need
Something?
You know
Be there for you
And stuff like that
That makes me feel
Better
But you know

You can't do
Nothing

I wish I could change the past. You know what I'm saying. If I could change the past, I would.

JOE STRESS

I just got to give it time. Time comes, I do what I need to do. You know, job. Getting on with my life. My mother does die I've gotta get on. Do what I gotta do.

IT'S HARD AS HELL
THE PROBLEMS ON ME
IS LIKE
I'M ALWAYS GONNA
BE THERE FOR
MY MOTHER
SITUATIONS LIKE
LOSING HER
MAKES ME FEEL
UNHAPPY
NOW THAT MY
DAUGHTER'S BORN
SHE FEELS MORE HAPPY
BECAUSE SHE FEELS GOOD
THAT AT LEAST
BEFORE SHE DIED
SHE LEFT SOMETHING
THAT'S ONE THING
SHE GONNA MISS
MY DAUGHTER
SHE CAN'T
TAKE CARE OF THE BABY
SHE GOT BACK PAINS AND
STUFF LIKE THAT
SO SHE CAN'T
THE BABY CRIES
TOO MUCH
MY MOTHER BE
FLIPPING OUT
I BE LIKE
OHHH!

I'm just sick and
Tired
Of all this hassling
All this pain
It bothers me
I can't take
No more

My Moms
She be bugging out
She's flipping
It's not the drugs
It's the sickness
It's messing her head
She starts swinging
On me
For little things
I be flipping out
Sometimes
I be cursing at her
So she get mad
She's just like
Getting on my nerves

Gloria thinks she got a ball going for her, leaving the baby with me on the weekends. Next week, I'm gonna be, like, "Yo, don't even think about bringing the baby." Cause I can't take the baby crying. I cannot take that. That bothers me. It's a pain. And I get mad.

Sometimes I feel like strangling the baby. I try to see what's wrong with her. Baby don't talk. Baby don't tell me what's going on. So. Baby stays quiet with her. Shit. She stays quiet with me, but at certain points, she fights sleep. When she's fighting sleep, I just be like, I wish I was you. I would've fell out a long time ago. I would've been ZZZZZZ.

I'm living with my mother again now. Things is hard because, she yells. She don't know what she's doing sometimes. AIDS is like a walking time bomb. It's really getting to her. It's already affected her mind. To me it hurts, to see my mother go through this. Because, now as more that I live with her, I understand what she's going through. She can't hear well. The doctors give her medicine. Some medicine she takes. Some she don't. She's trying. She still lives on. She can't stay in the bed sick all day. That's the one good thing about my mother. She got a lot of will power.

One time she was in the hospital, she stayed in there for like three months. And she lost a lot of weight while she was in. Then she came out and she gained a lot of weight. Now it's like, we're back together and she's doing as much as she could. She cooks, she cleans. She makes sure my clothes are clean. She makes sure my room is clean. Which I tell her, don't go into my room. It's that, she goes in there and she starts switching things around. And I'm like, Ma, where's this? Ma, where's that? I know where I put my stuff, so I shouldn't have a problem. She always does this to me.

I've really got a lot of stress on me. I don't get mad, because you know she does it for me. But, it's like sometimes, I tell her don't go in there, because no matter what, you sick and shit and you getting up and you doing such and such things. But I'd rather see her up than laying down. She'll get even more sick, just laying down. So I'd rather her still be doing something. She feel more better anyway when she's doing something.

It's been a couple of months
I was sick
I didn't feel good
Like today
Last night
My Mom took care of me
I came home
Did some homework,
Then went inside and laid down in bed.
I started coughing a lot
By twelve o'clock she came into my room
Here
Here's some cough drop
From there she gave me some juice
She came back around three
She gave me again
And she gave me some aspirin
I drank that
And at five she gave me again

Like that
She's like taking care of me
She's doing it because
She feels she should
I feel good because
That's my mother
And it's been a long time
Since I had felt that
She's giving me love
Know what I'm saying?

I like doing whatever I like to do. So, you don't bother me, I won't bother you. She stands in my way in a lot of things, and I get mad. She be flipping cause people be knocking on my door. It's that, they always go pick me up like that before we chill. They be calling me up. Girls and stuff like that.

See my thing is, I like to chill and just watch tv. Hang out. You know, enjoy myself. Usually that's what I like to do when I come out of work and school. I do my thing on the DL, on the down low. What you want me to do? Like, when I eat, I don't be washing my dish. I did what I did already, so why should I do more? And my mother, sometimes she doesn't understand it, so I get mad, and I, you know, I hurt her. She gets me mad. I mean mad. I hurt her feelings. I don't touch her. I try my best to get her. She be flipping. I know how to get her mad. Cause, you know, when I try to not get her mad, I get her mad anyway. The problem's the disease and all that.

My mother goes
What happened to you?
You used to never have
An attitude like this
Now you're different
Then I go
Well
The things you put me through
It gets to where
I'm gonna have
An attitude
She fucked up my life!
Don't have no life
Trying to make mine
And she fucked up
Can't stand that
Try to do my best
And always

I get
Fucked
Over

Joe's Themes

"I Do My Thing On The Down Low, The DL."

People are going to stand in your way, so you've got to lay low, sneak around, humor them, lie to them, whatever it takes. It doesn't make sense to tell them the truth, because then they're just going to mess with you, and you won't be able to get what you want.

Doing something on the DL, the down low, means to do it secretively. The concept of doing his thing on the DL expressed Joe's disregard of limits he felt interfered with what he wanted to do, while still, on the face of things, following the rules. The fact that these rules may have been made by people he cared about seemed to have little bearing on his decision not to abide by them. It was nothing personal, not so much a conflict with authority as a disregard of it.

Even when he was caught breaking the rules, as when Gloria became pregnant, Joe felt it was still best to continue lying so as not to get into more trouble. He was incensed when Gloria told Sarah how old she really was, even though Sarah forgave him. He attributed his problems with Sarah, not to his transgression, but to the fact that Gloria had told her the truth.

Joe expressed the tension between subterfuge and outward compliance in operating on the DL with, "No matter what, I'm gonna do mines. But I ain't gonna try to fuck up." Joe was determined to continue to bring girls to his room if he went back to live at the Center, but he would try to be better at concealing them because he didn't want to jeopardize his living situation or make Sarah angry. He didn't seem to consider the option of sacrificing his clandestine activity in order to comply with the rules, nor did he see any benefit for himself in compliance, beyond placating Sarah. The question for him was not whether he would follow the rules in order to return, but how he could circumvent the rules so as not to compromise his living situation or his desires.

The DL implies not just the covert, desired activity, but also the overt activity, intended to cover up what's happening on the down low. For Joe, this surface activity was often his well cultivated, albeit sometimes manipulative politeness. He described how he placated Sarah by apologizing for roughhousing then asking, "May I be excused?" The formality of his request may have appealed to Sarah with the respect and submission it implied. I found Joe to be extremely polite. He asked if he could smoke during the interview (which he did, despite a very persistent and severe cough), and he thanked me for a dinner and dessert I'd bought him, even though the food appeared to make his stomach hurt.

In a sense, much of the milieu in which Joe grew up was on the DL. This was due to the illegality of his mother's longstanding drug habit and her drug dealing. The legal system considers drug abuse a crime rather than an illness on the part of the abuser. This situation makes duplicity a necessity for addicts' self preservation. It can also affect their children, both as they model their parent's behavior and as they try to protect them. Joe was vague on details of his mother's drug use, despite the fact that he told me she had always used drugs. Perhaps his lack of awareness had been cultivated for her protection.

Living on the DL bred estrangement from "the system", and when problems arose the system was not seen as a resource or appealed to for help. Neither Joe nor those around him looked to the Child Welfare Agency when he was being beaten by Milagros. It was Joe's mother who intervened from jail and found alternate arrangements. When there were official interventions, they were often punitive, such as when Joe was sent to a group home and when his mother was incarcerated.

When Joe did seek outside help it was from the Center, an informal community center which provided space for self help groups and an unlicensed residence for teenagers. He was drawn there by the presence of other teenagers who came from family situations like his.

"I Don't Like To Tell About It."

Some things are too painful to talk about. Why bother, because it won't change anything anyway.

When a topic was too painful Joe declined to talk to me about it, and he indicated that he did this in other settings too. Topics Joe didn't want to talk about included his sojourn in a group home at age eight, which he stated was due to his mother's illness but intimated was related to "how your parents didn't stick." Another painful topic was being put out of his aunt's house for acting out when his mother was first put in jail. He told me he "felt like being bad" because he felt his aunt did not like him. When I asked him what had happened he told me, "It's personal. I don't like to tell about it." Even when he did choose to discuss sensitive topics with me he was often vague about the details, filling in the gaps with expressions like, "Something like that."

Joe dealt with arguments with his mother by walking out and not discussing the problem. Given the intractability of her drug addiction, maybe this was all he could do. Joe also told me how he did not want to argue with his girlfriend, which seemed to be a continuation of his desire to avoid painful topics.

Talking didn't help. It only brought up painful feelings, and it couldn't change the facts. This was true for his mother's addiction, her incarceration, and especially her AIDS. Joe said it was hard to talk about mother's AIDS because of its irreversibility. It had already happened and couldn't be changed, no matter how much he wished it could.

There was an exception to Joe's reluctance to talk about his problems. He told me he talked in the Addicted Teens Anonymous group at Center with other adolescents from chemically dependent families. He said that he felt understood and supported by the group there. He also indicated that the openness to talking about AIDS helped him to understand and begin to accept his mother's illness.

"I Was Going From House To House."

Joe experienced a great deal of instability in his life. Like the motherless children of the song, he was "wandering 'round from door to door." Before his mother went to jail he was sent to live in a group home, a very painful experience for him. He also stayed with his aunt, and when his mother went with her boyfriend to Puerto Rico, she left him with "some people" he didn't know, who robbed his house.

For the most part, Joe's caretakers exhibited a pattern of lack of understanding, neglect, and outright abuse. Although he did not voice any objections to his mother's care, she does not appear to have set consistent rules for him when he was young. He told me that one thing he liked about his mother was that, "when I was young, she used to let me go outside whenever I wanted." After her incarceration, Joe lived at first with his natural aunt, who does not appear to have understood the terrible strain he was under and threw him out after he acted out against her. He then went to live with the abusive Milagros, then with Gladys for a five year period of stability. When his mother was released he lived with her for a time, then at the Center, then back with his mother. He was planning to move back to the Center when I interviewed him.

The extended family did not provide much support to Joe and his mother. Perhaps they were estranged because of his mother's drug habit. Although Joe stayed briefly with his aunt before and just after his mother's incarceration, they had no contact after she put him out of the house. "I don't really like her, cause she put me out of the house." He told me he had run into her just a few weeks before our first interview. He wasn't sure who she was, and greeted her with, "Excuse me, ain't you my aunt?"

To replace his absent family Joe created a de facto family. Although he was an only child, his best friend at the Center, Edwin became his "brother." Gladys, a stable and nurturing figure for him, became his aunt.

"I Don't Want to Be Sitting Like A Sucker."

Joe felt like people were going to take advantage of him or outright harm him. He expected the worst and usually got it. His mother hurt him because her illegal activity and resultant incarceration caused him dislocation and abuse. The people who were supposed to watch him when his mother was in Puerto Rico robbed his house. He felt his aunt didn't like him, and she threw him out of her house when he had no place to go. Milagros beat him for no reason that he could see, other than her meanness and drug use.

Joe's experiences seemed to have primed him to feel victimized and exploited. Although Sarah gave him room and board, he felt treated unfairly because she bought other Center residents clothes and made him buy his own. He understood that this was because he had a source of income, Supplemental Security Income, and the other residents did not. However, he still felt resentful. When he contracted crab lice after a casual sexual liaison, Joe was sure the girl he was with had purposely given them to him. His girlfriend Gloria was unfaithful to him, and although he was unfaithful to her as well, this did not detract from his keen feeling of betrayal. He also felt used by her because she had been leaving their two month old baby with him on weekends. He did not feel obligated to care for his child, but instead saw the baby's visits as an imposition on his freedom that only benefitted the baby's mother.

The theme Sitting Like a Sucker has a corollary, "I Couldn't Do Nothing About It", which expressed Joe's feeling of helplessness, something he had experienced repeatedly as a child. Bad things happened, but he had no ability to influence them. About his mother, he told me, "I knew that she was taking drugs (and selling them as well) when I was living with her, but I couldn't do anything, because I was so young." He "couldn't do nothing about", the robbery of his apartment by the people his mother had left him with. He was powerless to stop Milagros from beating him. The best he could do was try to stay out of the way, mind his own business and watch cartoons.

The ultimate experience of helplessness was Joe's impotence in the face of his mother's illness and impending death. "What can I do? I can't do nothing." and "The bad thing about it is you can't do nothing. It's already happened."

"You Mess with Me, and I'll Catch You on the Down Low."

When things were going well Joe was sweet and mannerly. However, he was easily hurt when things did not go his way. He seemed to expect the worst and felt people purposely wanted to take advantage of him. When this happened he felt powerless and stupid and wanted to get back. Retaliation was a way of feeling like he had the upper hand in dealing with the people who had hurt him.

While it usually only made things worse, it gave Joe some satisfaction and a feeling of control.

When his girlfriend flirted with other boys while she was with him he told her, "You want to play yourself? Check this out!" and flirted aggressively with other girls. After she was unfaithful to him he told her, "You fuck with me, I'm going to make you feel fucking stupid", and had sex with her friend. He also retaliated against his mother's tirades by purposely getting her angry.

"Goody"

While Joe lashed out when he felt unliked or victimized, given positive regard he flourished. When his living situation was stable and he was adequately cared for, Joe developed his abilities and felt good about himself. The five years he lived with Gladys were a halcyon time for him. He attended school regularly, passed his classes and held a job. Most importantly, he felt good about himself. "Dag man, I was good when I was in 6th to 9th grade. I did everything as good as possible."

In spite of his admittedly wild and at times criminal behavior while staying at the Center, the positive regard he felt from Sarah contributed to his feeling that he was a good person. He even coined a nickname that celebrated his intrinsic goodness. "She always considered me one of the goodest ones. I consider myself Goody." Goody became his "thing", an identity that expressed his positive self esteem and gave him cachet and recognition.

Joe felt important and hip to be accepted as a part of the peer group at the Center. He particularly enjoyed dancing at the weekend disco. He derived a great deal of satisfaction from the release of tension dancing offered him, as well as from the recognition of his ability by his peers, and even from *The New York Times*.

"The Mack"

A major part of Joe's self image was the mack, a ladies man. Joe declared wholeheartedly, "I love girls!" and he appeared to spend a great deal of energy pursuing them. Girls were like a stimulant, euphoric substance for him. He seemed to equate being good with the ability to attract girls, while not having girlfriends tapped into feelings of being bad and inadequate. Perhaps he tried to compensate for feeling "dissed" and deficient when he was younger by flirting aggressively and having multiple sex partners to prove his desirability. He pointedly told me that he always got more girls than his friend Edwin. His focus on girls may have served to help him forget his other problems.

"The mack" also has the connotation of being a pimp. Some of Joe's scheming to get girls into his room at the Center had an impersonal, predatory quality. He described how he lied to Sarah to get the girl upstairs, then would, "Jump all up in her skin," and have sex with her. He clearly enjoyed being in control. It was hard to let go of those feelings, and he seemed let down when the tryst ended. He told me he was "sad to see [the girls] go" when they left.

Joe was proud of the fact he'd had sex with a lot of girls. When I asked him about condoms he said people should use condoms. He told me he didn't use them with his girlfriend Gloria because they were in love and later admitted he didn't always use them with other girls either. He worried about this, but since neither he nor Gloria had contracted a major sexually transmitted disease, his worries were temporarily assuaged.

"Gonna Be a Different Day."

"I think about tomorrow all the time . . . get to the next day. Cause the next day's gonna be a different day."

Joe looked to the future for hope, not for any specific goal, but in a desire for change, to escape the present. He was not certain tomorrow would be better, but at least it would be different. Anything had to be better than today. But when tomorrow came he was still looking for the next day after.

Joe tried to hope, but it was hard, and his experience had taught him to doubt. He was initially inspired by a story he read for homework about a Puerto Rican man who made it despite adversity. He identified with the man and was touched by his story. It briefly gave him hope that he could make it too. But then he stated that he and the man were not really alike. Perhaps the man did not have to deal with AIDS, maybe not with a drug addicted mother. Joe decided that the story, "could be a lie".

Joe occasionally took some comfort from the thought that he would prevail in the long run. He hoped for an ultimate justice when those who had hurt him and gained at his expense would ultimately lose. He hoped he would come out on top, even though he had been taken advantage of initially. This perspective enabled him to preserve some degree of optimism and selflessness without feeling like a fool.

"I got a heart too. I care about other people. Even though people do mess with my feelings. And I do get hurt. But (brightly) I don't let it stress me, because, just like a person who's trying to steal from me, I be like, yo, you steal from me. You lost. You might get paid off of it, but in the long run I will get more out of it."

However, it was hard for him to sustain this feeling. He said it so brightly, that I got the feeling he didn't fully believe how, or if, this would really happen.

"In a Way, My Mother Ruined My Life, But in Another Way, She Didn't."

Joe's relationship with his mother was characterized by deep ambivalence. On the one hand, Joe felt a great deal of anger towards his mother: She had brought him dislocation and suffering because of her drug addiction, incarceration and illness. "Try to do my best and always I get fucked over . . . She fucked up my life".

At the time of our interviews Joe told me that most of their conflict centered around cleaning his room. He was alternately understanding and infuriated at her incursions into his room. He got back at her by purposely getting her angry. He told me ironically that he could do that even when he wasn't trying.

Several weeks after my last interview with him, Sarah told me that Joe's mother had been using drugs again for quite some time. In fact, Joe and his mother were facing eviction because she had not paid the rent in three months. Sarah speculated that she was using the money for drugs. Joe didn't tell me she was using drugs again, nor that this was an area of conflict. Maybe her drug use was off limits because it was so hopeless.

In spite of the fact that she had caused him a great deal of pain and disrupted his life because of her use of drug use, Joe loved his mother. He was happy and receptive to her solicitous care when he was sick. "She's taking care of me. I feel good cause that's my mother. It's been a long time since I had felt that. She's giving me love".

"The Sickness Is Messing Her Head."

"My moms be bugging out. She's flipping. Not from the drugs, from the sickness."

Joe was witness to his mother's deterioration from AIDS. She behaved violently and unpredictably, "She starts swinging on me for little things". It was difficult for him to cope with her increasingly irrational behavior.

It was also painful for Joe to contemplate her death, because of the suffering and rootlessness it would bring. Even though his mother had failed to provide a stable, nurturing home, she had still been a fixed anchor point in his life. His father was not in his life at all, so when she died he would be without parents. Whatever her problems, he still felt loyalty to her because she was his mother. The uncertainty of when she would die and the uncertainty of what would become of him were particularly difficult for him to deal with.

Living with her had given Joe a realistic view of AIDS. He knew it is not an immediate death sentence, but he also saw the physical and mental devastation it wrought on his mother. Witnessing its ravages firsthand appeared to increase his dread of contracting the disease himself. However, his fear of the disease did not appear to promote consistently safe behavior, and he admitted to me instances of unsafe sex with girls other than Gloria. He never used a condom with her, despite knowing she was having unprotected sex with other partners.

"I Like to Chill."

Joe liked to relax by watching television and hanging out with his friends. He resented any intrusions into his leisure activities and did not see why he should have to do things like clean up after himself. He felt that his work study program was taxing enough. "I did what I did already. Why should I do more?" He did not want to take responsibility for anything other than his own pleasure.

Joe was ready to adopt a live and let live attitude towards others, "Don't bother me. I won't bother you". However, if demands were made on him, Joe retaliated. For example, he told me that he purposely angered his mother to get back at her for telling him to clean up after himself.

He experienced caring for his baby daughter as an unwelcome demand. Although he professed that he was taking responsibility for his baby, other than giving her his name, he did not appear to do much for her. He resented having to care for her on weekends and saw it as an imposition on his freedom and peace of mind. He saw no benefit for himself in spending time with her and instead felt used by the baby's mother.

"Something Now to Live For."

Joe maintained that he got his girlfriend Gloria pregnant by accident. He never used a condom with her because he felt love for her, but he did not seem to connect that with the likelihood that she might become pregnant.

Joe's first reaction to her pregnancy was to demand she have an abortion, but when she didn't he said he wanted to take responsibility for the baby. He legally affirmed paternity and gave the child his last name. At our first interview, about a month after her birth, Joe proudly received congratulations from other people at the Center while we talked and told me, "A lot of people see my daughter and say she's gorgeous . . . and it feels good! . . . I certainly have to cherish that. Cause I got something now to live for."

He felt that his daughter also made his mother feel good. "Now that my daughter's born, my mother feels more happy, because she feels good, that at least before she died she left something".

While the idea of the baby instilled pride and solace, the reality of the baby's needs and his inability to meet them were terribly frustrating. Neither he nor his mother seemed able to cope with the baby, and his mother's erratic behavior only exacerbated the situation. It made him furious that the baby cried. By our second interview, only three weeks after the first, Joe told me, "I can't take the baby crying. Sometimes I feel like strangling the baby".

Joe had free access to his daughter, but he didn't seem to want to see her at all. He was angry that the baby's mother had been dropping her off with him on weekends. He had worried from the outset that Gloria might try to manipulate him with the baby, and he felt used by her. He told me he planned to tell her to stop bringing the baby to him. He preferred to come to her to see the baby when he wanted.

While the ideal of a baby might have seemed like something to live for and to give solace to his dying mother, the reality of the baby's needs and Joe's and his mother's inability to cope with her were a source of great frustration. She had symbolized hope for him at the outset, but it was a very tenuous hope considering how quickly his response to her had soured from pride to rage.

MARIA

When I got to the Center to meet Maria for the first time the man at the upstairs reception desk called out her name. A girl with her head on a table behind him looked up. I spoke her name, and she gave me a faint smile and then stood up, revealing a big belly poking out over baggy jeans held up by a belt. She lurched forward and almost fell over. I helped her to regain her balance, and she muttered that she was tired, indicating her pregnant belly. I wondered if she was high.

Maria said she had to go to the bathroom, and as I waited for her I looked around. It was very dark, and in an alcove there was a television tuned to cartoons surrounded on three sides by couches strewn with inert forms. Behind the reception desk was another television, which was tuned to talking heads and which no one was watching.

Maria started off very slowly, hardly speaking. Throughout much of the interview she spoke haltingly. I often had to probe gently to get her to elaborate. Sometimes she spoke with a sweetness and animation which made me feel close to her, like she was confiding in me. Occasionally she smiled, a dazzling, clear, healthy smile, which made her look strong and self assured.

As she talked Maria alternated between looking strong, clear and direct and looking tired, with dark circles under her eyes and her head hanging loosely. Although she told me some heartrending things, such as how she'd learned of the deaths of her father and later her mother, she never became overwhelmed by sadness. By contrast, when she spoke of her anger her manner became hard and belligerent.

While we talked people occasionally came into the gameroom. An adult named Junior, who looked like a staff person came through a few times. Joe came in, looking small and tired, and Maria bummed a cigarette. Junior came through and told her she should quit smoking. The next time he came through he kissed her. After a while he opened a small door to the ballroom and began playing loud music, setting up for the Friday night disco. At one point Maria got up to tell him to turn it down. He explained he had only a short time left to do it, and she said she had only a few minutes as well. He kept the music on and she returned, still walking erect with her head up and smiling, even in defeat.

After I turned off the tape recorder Maria said she was interested in the fact that I was getting a doctorate. She wanted to be an obstetrician. In fact she would be a midwife. She could do that with less schooling, and it was just as good. She said that she just hated to see children mistreated. I remembered her chilling comments about how she used to drop her younger brother Alfred on the floor when he was an infant because she was jealous of him.

After the interview she said she had to go to the bathroom and took me to Sarah's office, which was just off the gameroom. Joe and another boy were there. Sarah was laying on the side of the bed with her legs up, covered by a long skirt. She had on her black blouse with no collar. She had on no makeup and looked younger and more relaxed than she had the last time I saw her.

Sarah suggested I might want to look at the living room before I left. Maria and Joe took me up. Sarah had said that she'd cleaned it but someone's dog had defecated in it. The living room was painted orange with old but comfortable matching grey sofas, old bureaus and small sculptures. It looked very well thought out, informal, inexpensive, and tasteful. But there were several mounds of dog feces scattered around the floor. Joe said it stunk, and I asked who would clean it. No one said anything.

I met a tall young African-American man fixing his hair at the three-way mirror at the landing just outside the living room. He shook my hand and said his name was Ivan, but otherwise seemed uninterested in Maria and Joe. We returned to Sarah's, and I bid them goodbye and Merry Christmas, promising to meet with Maria in the new year.

Our second interview came around six weeks later. I got to the hotline on time, but Maria was not there yet. She had phoned the Center to say she was just leaving her step-father's apartment. The man at the desk told me I could sit and wait and waved toward a row of black plastic chairs against the wall opposite him. I sat on the last one, closest to the dark television room. About 12 people were sitting or lying there, watching a sitcom. No one spoke. Behind me was a blackboard with a list of tasks matched with names. In front of me were two desks with the man on reception duty and a woman talking quietly but intently at one. Raquel, a woman I had met on my first visit to the Center was on the phone at the other desk. She greeted me with a hi, and I returned the greeting. Behind the desks was a four-drawer filing cabinet, and a woman was sitting on the floor in front of it emptying papers, clothing and a video from the cabinet into a garbage bag.

Raquel had a short, mannish fade haircut and appeared to be wearing only a bathrobe, slippers, and a bead necklace. She got up and looked at a black garbage bag on the floor, asking whose things were in it. When no one responded, she asked for gloves. The woman at the reception desk opened a drawer and gave her a package of latex gloves. Raquel put them on and pulled clothing, pants and sweaters, from the bag. She ascertained they were a woman's clothes and then said they would have to be thrown away, since no one was claiming them. She announced a meeting in ten minutes and checked the duty roster.

When the meeting began the inert forms in the television room got up off the couches and pulled plastic chairs into the area I was sitting in. I did not want to intrude on the meeting, as the one I had sat in on previously was very intimate. I asked Raquel where I should sit, and she told me to sit on one of the couches in the television room. The lights there had been turned on, and the television was shut off. I went over to the far couch. I looked at its covering of a tucked in sheet, which was strewn with crumbs and pieces of dirt and hair. I felt uncomfortable. Many of the people who had been laying on it looked very unkempt. I wondered if anyone had lice. I made sure not to let my hair touch the couch and rested my coat halfway on my tote bag.

Maria came after about ten more minutes, forty minutes late, and we went into the gameroom. She wore jeans, a new looking football jersey and a leather coat. Her belly was very big. She walked slowly and appeared tired and distracted. Some boys and a girl came up to her, and she told them she'd be finished in an hour.

Maria ate sunflower seeds as she spoke, leaving the shells on a table beside us. She watched and periodically brushed away the roaches that persisted in exploring the area around the tape recorder and the shell pile. At one point she appeared to become angry and banged her fist on the table, scattering the shells and sending a roach running. Junior came by and offered her some bottled water, saying that she drank it sweetly. She did, using her top lip to slow down the flow to her mouth, unlike his guzzling. Maria was more reserved than last time, not getting as angry when she showed anger.

At the end of the interview she offered me some gum, then put on her coat and walked downstairs with me. She asked to see a picture of my children, but I had none with me. I told her that when we met again I would bring one. She said she was going to stay at the Center. I gave her a hug, which she reciprocated, and wished her good luck. I later wrote a poem about her.

Maria

Belly bursting
Ripe
Life is in me.
Life
I grab for it
Wrap myself around it
Like Bambu[1] around weed[2]
Holding in the pleasure
Before it goes up in smoke.
I grab for it
But the ghosts are in my way
Blocking me
Mocking me.
Death
How could it happen to Mommy?
Death
It will not happen to me.
In the dark alley of my days
I grab for life.
I grab for it in a kiss,
Wet, and never enough;
In a fight,
Stinging reminder that I am;
In a Blunt,[3]
Brief pleasure until the ghosts return
Haunting me
Taunting me.
Only my baby can fill me
And save me from the emptiness of death.

Notes:
1: Bambu is paper used to roll marijuana cigarettes
2: Weed is marijuana
3: A Blunt is a marijuana cigarette

Maria's Story

I came to the Center when I was 14. I ran away from home because me and my
mother weren't getting along. I mean, I wanted to live with her, but I couldn't.

Cause we always fight. We never got along, because I'm just like her, attitude
wise.
My mother's always been angry
She's not trying to hear from anybody
She's right and
That's it
It's what I say goes
Not what I do
I feel that if you want me
To do as you say
Then
You do as you say!
I mean
How can you be a role model to me and
Do something and
Tell me not to do it?
How you go taking drugs
And telling me
I can't do it
I'm gonna do it!
If you did it
Why can't I do it?
It's not that I want to do it
That's what I was telling her
But if you expect me to
Follow that good example,
Show me
Instead of doing the opposite
That's stupid
And then she get mad
"Oh, you think you're smart
You think you know it all
What the fuck you thinking bitch?"
Call me a bitch
And I hate that word
Bitch
"Who you calling a bitch?"
Then right away we start fighting
We can't be around each other
   I wasn't holding my tongue. I'll say whatever I feel like. If I was angry I
would say it. And she thought it was disrespectful because she was my mother.

But why should I hold my tongue? If I feel something, I'm gonna let you know.
And she can't deal with that. I was just like her.

I have so much anger
I'm ready to just hurt anybody
That's how my mother was
She wanna eat your ass
She's bad
I mean my mother was
A lovely person
If you in need
She help you
But she just
Had her feelings
I guess it was something
She couldn't deal with
So she found
Other ways
To deal with it

I started hating her
Because she did drugs
Heroin
And when she did them
The way she would treat me
She used to abuse me!
Punch me
Pull my hair
Kick me
I thought
It was just that
She hated me
But it was
The drugs
One minute she'd be
Up
Next minute she'd be
Down
I thought it was normal
I didn't know

My mother always, she's been there physically, but not mentally. She was
in another world. She went from a good job to nothing. I seen the difference. She

always kept herself clean, and I guess you really couldn't tell she was using drugs. But then she lost her job, and she just started bugging out when my brother was born. Not Alfred. He's 12 or 13. I had another brother. He would've been about eight now. But he died when he was a baby. He was four months old. I was 11 when he died. I didn't know it, but he had AIDS. I only knew he died cause he was sick.

Then when I was going on 13
My father told me he had AIDS
He was dying from it
And he told me right before he died
He used drugs
Which I already knew
He told me to stay away from drugs
That God's gonna forgive him
That he's sorry
And he hopes I forgive him
Cause he's done bad things to me
He was just apologizing I guess
What could I say?
I didn't say anything
I just stood there and listened
Cried
I felt bad

And then, when he died, my mother stopped using drugs. Cold turkey. She disappeared for like two weeks. She got sick, and she put herself in the hospital. But she didn't tell anybody, so, nobody knew where she was at. I was living with my grandmother. We had gotten evicted from our apartment because my parents were selling drugs there. I had an idea about the drugs, but I wasn't really sure because, I really never seen the drug exchange. Or drug use. But I knew it was something. That's when life started getting a little difficult. Well, actually a lot. I started holding resentments. Against both, but mostly my mother. Cause, she lived and my father didn't. I wish they both lived.

My mother wasn't sick
When she died.
She died from stress
I guess
Cause after my father died
She stopped drugs
She started going to school
Working
Wearing herself out

The doctor used to tell her
She can't overwork herself
But my mother had to
Keep herself occupied
She was doing a lot of things
She always was tired
From staying up
Doing term papers
Cooking
Making sure my brother
And my stepsister
Went to bed
Just
She doing things
Going visiting my Grandmother
Making up to her for what she did
She felt guilty I guess
So she tried to change her
Whole life around
It killed her
It finally took her

My mother would not talk to me about anything for nothing. I would try, but she wouldn't talk. My father, he'd go, this is how it was, this is how it is, and this is how it's gonna be. The end.

My mother wasn't like that. She kept everything balled up inside. If she wasn't so scared, she would've ran and took the AIDS test. But she couldn't.

That's how I figured it. I mean, if she's giving birth to a baby that's born with the virus, how could she not have the virus? She was just living in denial. That living in denial kept her angry. So, her being angry, she had to keep herself occupied. So, her keeping herself occupied stressed her out. She was trying not to think about it. I guess she figured it wasn't supposed to happen to her. But it does. They say AIDS doesn't discriminate.

She didn't take the AIDS test. She was scared to. What she died of is confidential, cause it's not in her death certificate. Like it is in my father's? Hers just says that she died of natural causes. She was 37.

I would say she's, not a liar but, times I asked her about AIDS, she just said no. It was just a front. You know what I'm saying? Half the people, they be all cheery in the face,

MARIA DISCLOSURE

while hurting deep down inside. Especially when it's family. Families are supposed to know. You're supposed to tell your kid what's going on with you. It goes both ways. Just like you have a right to know what's happening with your kid? Maybe your kid has every right to know about you too. That's how I see it. Me and my father proved it. Just the same way he had every right to know about me, he thought I had every right to know about him.

All I wanted her to do was to tell me. Like my father did. But everybody's not the same. She just didn't want to face reality. That she had it. And being that she was leaving my little brother Alfred behind, it must have scared her more. Then again, I turned out very fine, and I was small when my father died. I mean, I ain't the greatest kid around but, I turned out pretty well from a lot of other people that grew up. Who feel sorry for themselves. Who become drug addicts themselves. And, they go out and end up in jail. Prostitution and stuff like that.

She just didn't say
Nothing

Come on with that
Shit!
How you gonna sit there
You know that you're
Sick
You're dying
And just look at your kid
With a straight face
Act like nothing
Have no guilty feelings
Whatsoever that's
Eating you?
Why don't you just
Blow up and
Say it?
SHE JUST
COULDN'T DO IT
AND THE MORE
SHE COULDN'T DO IT
THE MORE
I COULDN'T TAKE IT

I KNEW. I JUST WANTED HER TO TELL ME. I JUST WAITED AND WAITED. THE MORE I WAITED, THE ANGRIER I GOT.

I couldn't see how she could sit there in my face and not tell me. Me being her daughter. What am I gonna do? Leave you? Abandon you? You my mother. You brought me into this world. You tell me that you're sick, I'm gonna, "Okay, bye." Come on! I didn't leave my father.

She just didn't want to. She'd turn her head and act like she didn't hear me. I'd tell her, you ever thought about taking the AIDS test? She said nah. And I know she had AIDS. And I knew she knew she had AIDS. She was just scared to find out. And I always said when she dies I ain't gonna be crying. I won't feel it.

When she died I felt it. I knew she was dead. I felt something was wrong. She was in the hospital for two weeks before she died. I was living at the Center. I was sleeping, right? And I was dreaming about her, about fighting with her. At the Center there was an intercom on the phone. And through the intercom I heard, "Maria, emergency. Call your house."
I knew right then and there
I looked down at the floor
Should I phone
Or shouldn't I?
Then when I finally did pick up the phone
My heart was just like
Pounding and pounding and pounding
Really fast
And the phone's ringing
My stepsister picks up the phone
And I hear it in her voice
Maria come home now
You gotta come home!
Why? What happened?
But I knew
I felt it
And I'm saying to myself
It's true?
Oh God
Please no!
Please don't do this to me
Not now
And she just starts crying
Maria
Your mother's dead
I just dropped the phone
God
It was hurting so much!
And I couldn't say it
I just sat there crying
My friend looked at me and said, "It happened, right?" I was like, "She's dead." I had just finished seeing her the day before! She looked tired. Like, sleepy tired? But not totally, pale and everything. Just tired.
I got dressed and went to my house. My stepfather opened the door, and he looked at me. He thinks I look too much like my mother. He just looked at me, and (whispers) he starts crying. I didn't know what to do! I hadn't been to my

house in so long. Cause me and my mother were fighting. I just didn't know what to do. And my little brother didn't know yet. (Whispers) I was just crying and crying. Finally, I go to my grandmother's house, and everybody's trying to figure a way how to tell my brother. So I said, "Tell him the way y'all told me. Your father's dead." You know. That's how they told me, when my father died. They came to my school and told me.

The minute my father died, I felt it too. I was 12 years old. I was gonna cut out of school, to go smoke a blunt? And something told me, "Don't cut. Go back to school." I felt it. I told my friends, "Yo. I don't know what it is, but I have to go back." And as soon as I set foot in the school, I heard the intercom, "Maria Rivera report to the guidance office." I was like, (whispers) "No!" I felt it. I knew it was coming, but I didn't know what it was. I felt him go. The second I left the school, I felt something, in me. And that was when he died.

I walked in
And my guidance counselor looked at me
She told me
Sit down
I said
I ain't gonna be sitting
Cause I know
Right then I started flipping
I punched the window and broke it out
With my hand!
Then I wrecked the guidance counselor's office with a chair
I just started flipping
My grandmother came and took me to her house
I locked myself in the bathroom
I broke the wall in the bathroom
I pulled the toilet seat off the toilet
And I pulled down the shower curtain
They left me
Because they knew
The best thing to do is stay away from me

The way I was with my father was the way my brother was with my mother. So, after my mother died they were like, "How we gonna tell Alfred?" When Daddy died, Alfred was still young. Daddy's death changed my mother. That's when she stopped drugs. So, Alfred got treated better. My mother treated him the best, out of all of us.

Everywhere she went
He went
Everything we got

He got
Everything we didn't get
He got
I mean everything
She hardly slapped him around
She hit him when he needed to be hit
Not like us
If she was high
She'd just hit us

I really used to hate my brother. When he was a baby, me being like, jealous, I used to beat him up. I actually did it on purpose. I did a lot of bad things to him. I used to (quietly, almost conspiratorially) drop him, and slap him around. I was little too, seven, eight, nine. I was just, evil. I knew I was angry because he got treated better than me. But I just, didn't care.

As I got older, I started realizing, he's just a little kid. And my mother wasn't on drugs, so he got treated better. I learned to accept, that's my little brother. Even though he's a pain. I give him whatever I could. I'll slap him if he deserves to be slapped. He's shit scared of me. He will not put his hands on me. I say, I'll knock your ass across that room. I don't like beating. I slap. You know, I bang him on his arm. I'm not your mother. But I feel like, I'm the oldest in this house. And you're gonna respect what I say. You don't talk back to me. Cause if you ask me to buy you this and buy you that, then you can also do what you're supposed to do and listen.

I was trying to explain to Alfred
About Mommy
So he could understand
My mother did what she did
But she loved us!
She tried her best
I told him
At that time
That's what people did
Heroin
Just like now
People smoke crack
They smoke weed and sniff coke
Then there was heroin and mescalin tabs
Mommy wasn't strong enough
She didn't have that
Will power
And she got caught up in it

I'm pretty sure she regretted it

My stepfather was telling me, "Don't tell him that." I'm not gonna lie to my brother! (angrily) I'm gonna tell him straight up. The facts. He has to know, one way or the other. Maybe you and my mother lied to me. But I'm not gonna lie to my brother. My grandmother said, just because you had a bad experience, and Alfredo didn't, don't make him see a side that he never saw, of your mother. Me and my sister saw a side that we shouldn't of saw. Our mother had problems that she couldn't deal with, that led her to do what she did. I said, I'm not trying to make him feel miserable or look down on Mommy. I'm just letting him know.

People ask me

Your parents are dead?

I don't give a fuck

I say

You got a problem with that?

Shuh

They ain't saying nothing to me

You know what I'm saying?

I'll tell them if I feel like it

If I don't feel like telling you

I'll say mind your business

If I want to tell you I'm telling

But not just telling anybody

Some of us say it with no problem

We say what we gotta say

Some kids just keep to themselves about it

Cause maybe it's

Too much of a burden on them

It was hard when they died. I want them to be here. But, that's life. That's just one of, God's choices, to take my parents. So He took them. That's what my grandmother says. I just say they died cause they were sick. (wan laugh)

I don't know if there's a heaven or hell. I think they're just dead. Sometimes I feel, mmm, maybe there's a God, maybe not. But I don't actually believe there's a God. No, I ain't seen him. I didn't touch him yesterday, and I don't know. And that fucking roach keeps coming back! (smacks the table hard) Right? (very quietly) I don't know, really. I don't know! It's just that. Maybe I want it to be.

Every time I get angry and frustrated

Where I feel I'm

Out of control

I go outside and actually

Physically hurt somebody

I can't do that
I'm getting older
I have to find some way to deal with it
I'm pregnant now
Somebody might hit me back
I don't care
But I got to look out for my kid

I remember when I was pregnant the last time. I was so angry, I couldn't think straight. I just, exploded. I started pow, punching my stomach. And right then and there I knew, I can't have this baby. I had an abortion. Because, there I was, 16, no parents. My mother was alive then, but, to me she wasn't my mother. She wasn't using drugs, but she was just up with herself, in her own world. She flipped out. She was screaming and crying. "How could you do this! You need to be locked up, to do this to me. I just can't believe you'd do something like this." And I didn't mean to! It was a one night stand. I used a condom, but it broke.

I didn't want to be pregnant this time either. I really had thoughts. Even now, I still do. Damn. In the beginning I wanted it. Then, when I hit five months, I was going through this little stage where I couldn't take it. I wanted to get rid of it. But I dealt with it. I figure, why not. I just didn't let myself get too upset over things. Like whether my mother wanted me to have this baby. My mother had just died. Or did God want me? Cause I'm atheist. I don't believe in God.
I had a lot of things going through my head
I felt like
I was going to be by myself
I don't want to be . . .
You know
I don't care
Nobody wants to be there to help me with anything
The hell with you!
I figure I can do it by myself
I know it's going to be hard
But I can try
I used to think
I can't have this baby
Because I have no patience
I won't be able to handle it
But then
For some reason
Somebody was there with me
Somebody was over my shoulder

My father
And my mother
Probably them both
But I know there was
Somebody over my shoulder
Because if I really felt I couldn't handle it
I would've had the abortion
But I just didn't
    My mother had my sister at the age of 16. She was like, "I had a baby when
I was young. Don't do it. It's gonna mess up your whole life."
But I now feel that
My mother's not here
She wanted me to have this baby
Because
It's going to be a girl
To replace her
You understand?
Or if it's a boy
To replace my father
It's not like my parents
But,
Just to have something there
Cause I'm here by myself
The baby
That's your mother
Being with you
Or
Your father
Cause that's family
I'm not talking about
Cousins
I'm talking about
Mother
Brother
Sister
I just feel like
My mother had something to do with it
Because she ain't here to help me (very quietly)
    I want to have something there. Cause I'm here by myself. I mean, I have
my little brother, but I'm older than he is, and he's looking up to me if anything.
I need somebody to look up to. So maybe this, maybe having a baby will change

something. It will be something to help me change my life, by not being so damn lazy. Cause I'm lazy! There's times I don't go to school. I won't clean. I just don't do anything. If I don't have to do it, I won't do it. It's that I don't have the responsibility. In ways, my mother wanted me to have it. She's the one that told me to have my baby. Think about it. You lose one, you gain another. Easy come, easy go. I'm going to name her Vanessa Carmen. My mother's name was Carmen.

I know it's not gonna be easy. Cause when you babysit somebody else's kids you feel like (snarls and laughs). Only, you got to go through it sometime. So I'd rather go through it now. I know when people get smacked around they can end up smacking their own kids. But when you know it's yours, you treat it different. I would treat my kid better than I would treat you. That's being cherished, not slapped around and starved. If I ever can't control myself, I can't say, cause I let it boil up before I hit. I stop myself a lot of times before I keep hitting. Believe me, I stop myself. Cause there are times, when I felt like, I even thought to myself, "Maria, I wonder how it would be if I just, got rid of him." You know. My stepfather. But that's insane. I feel bad, cause, he's my folks.

I guess I feel like, I don't know. Down and out the majority of the time. So I just stay home. I feel the same way there, but it's away from people. I don't have to say anything. Just watch some tv. Eat. And just think. Sit there and think. I don't do drugs. Well, okay, once in a while I'll smoke a blunt. You know what that is? Marijuana. But I don't drink. I haven't drunk since I got pregnant. I haven't drunk in so long. I think if I took a sip of beer (makes a sick face) But, I used to drink. Every summer, I'd be right outside. All night, til like three or four in the morning, getting drunk. 40's, meth, blunts. I didn't give a fuck.

I guess I smoke weed
When I feel like
Really
Like I can't take it (sighs)
I feel down and out
Then I'll smoke and
I'll just sit there and
I'm high
So
I'll think
I'm always sorry
(gestures at her belly)
You know
Cause
I know
But sometimes
I FEEL I HAVE TO!
See I'm that type
When I get really
Frustrated
Down and out
I go and I
Flip on somebody
Anybody
I punch walls

MARIA
DRUGS

My mother
She had a choice
The same way like me
I have a choice
The same way
With smoking pot
I choose to do it
Cause I want to!
It's there
And I'll do it
Same way she

I see the people around me. See, I grew up with this kid. We lived in the same building. His mother and my mother and father were using drugs together. You know what I'm saying. And now his mother mad sick. You see her and she's sick, but she doesn't care.

She still getting high
I see her and be like
Dag
People on who are on
Drugs
Ask for death
She have the choice
To stop
She just
Don't give a fuck
So why should
She live?
God should take her
Away

But He takes the people
Who changed their lives
My mother's
Not the only one
There's a lot of other
People who've
Changed their lives
Stopped using drugs
And died!

And there's people that's
Still using drugs
And still living!
Walking around
I'm not saying that lady
Deserves to die
What I'm saying is
If she knows she's sick
She's supposed to
Keep herself healthy
To live
She don't wanna live cause
She's still choosing to
Use drugs
Then why is she
Still walking?
For that God should be
"Oh well then"
Not that I'm saying that
They deserve it
But they just don't
Give a fuck

80% of the time
It works that way
The drug addict lives
And the people who
Quit drugs died
Drugs (sucks her teeth)
They say drugs kill you
I think drugs keep you
Alive

I mean people are still
Using drugs
And they dying
And they still alive!
These people who stop
Using drugs
Are dying
And are dead

I wouldn't shoot drugs. I don't even like, taking blood out. For any type of blood, anything, before they stick a needle, they need to tie my wrist down to the chair. Cause I will not let you stick no shit in my arm! I just scream.

Tomorrow I'm going to Virginia. If I like it I'll probably have my prenatal records transferred down there. But if I don't then I'll probably come back around Christmas. I'm really not sure. I never been down there. It's a last minute decision. Cause I'm going through some problems now. There's this boy, Ricky, that I'm in love with. The other day, he told me he feels it's better that we just not be together. And it hurt me. I started crying and stuff. That's why I'm leaving, cause I want to get away. I'd rather not deal with it. I rather just leave it alone.

Alright, how do I put this? Ben and I were together for like 5 years. Ricky and Ben are friends. I played Ben, with Ricky. I did it cause I wanted to, cause I like Ricky. After I did what I did with Ricky, I didn't get my period anymore. I just wasn't, you know, cautious. So, for the first 3 months, I was with Ricky and Ben. But then, after that, I just left Ben alone and I stood with Ricky. From the get go, I never told Ricky the baby was his. Everybody else thinks it's his. I'm the only one saying it's Ben's.

Ben says he hopes it's his. But Ricky expect me not to talk to Ben anymore. I tried to explain to him. If it is Ben's baby, how can I just not talk to him. That'll be his kid. He's gonna have to come see it. Well, not have to, cause at first I told Ben, I don't want to have nothing to do with you. Cause I wanted Ricky. You can't see your baby. Just, leave it at that. I didn't plan to get pregnant, it just happened. But being that I chose to keep the baby, I feel it's my decision, on what to do. But then I started thinking. Kids can't grow up with just one parent. It's not right. So I told Ben he can see the baby.

I tried to explain to Ricky. I'm not asking you to put out money to help me support my baby. I can do that on my own. You can leave whenever you want. I ain't gonna hold you back.
That's
Men's way of life
Ninety percent of men
Leave their children
To do whatever
Be with other women
A lot of parents today are single
Because the men
Just don't want to be there
You can easily pick up your shit and leave
It's hard for a mother to do that
Because I'm the one who's
Carrying the baby for 9 months
I'm the one who's
Gotta give birth to it

Your feelings towards the baby
Wouldn't be as close as mine
It's easy for you to leave
I won't hold you back either

I told Ricky, if I need something, you expect me not to talk to Ben. Where am I gonna get it from? You say you ain't gonna help me. What you rather me choose? To go out there and fuck somebody? Excuse my language. Or ask him? Being he's the father. Whatever runs through his head, I don't know. He doesn't talk to me or nothing. So, I'd rather not deal with it. I just want to get away for a little while. I told him, if you keep this up, your confusion and putting me through this pain, then by the time my baby comes, I ain't gonna want to be with you any more. Cause I'm gonna want to be with my kid. Then you're gonna want to be with me, and it's gonna be too late.

I told him
You're younger than
Me
You don't need a kid
You're not as
Responsible as I am
I've been in the
Streets
Since I was 12
I've done a lot of
Things to
Support myself
Not sexually
Not sleep around
With people
But sell drugs
Know what I'm saying?
I know street life
You've had your
Mother there
To buy you things
Pat you on your back
Wash your ass
I didn't have
Any parents to
Do that
So I know what it is
To be responsible

I'm not asking you to be
A father.
I don't ask him for Nothing
I bought my carriage
I bought my crib
I bought my playpen
From Welfare
Plus some money I had
Saved up from before
Now all I need is
Diapers and wipies
And some clothes
So I don't ask you for
Nothing
It's not like you have to Be
obligated to do Anything
If you choose to help me
Then that's on you

MARIA
SURVIVAL

Just like Ben
I don't ask him for
Nothing
Today he was like
What the baby needs?
The baby don't need
Nothing
I don't want
Nothing
From you
"Oh, why it gotta be
Like that?"
Cause that's how I feel
Well, if I need some-
thing
I'll ask you
If I desperately
Needed it
Because if the baby's
His
He should have to
Do for it
If I choose for him to
If I want it

I'm pregnant
That's why it makes it
Even harder
Cause you think
Damn!
I have to take care of
The baby somehow
Cause Welfare don't
Give you a lot
And damn
Should I just risk it?
Do what I got to do?
And
My kid will have
Or
Just let my kid
Do without?
Just as long as it
Has what it needs
You understand?

I know the street
I know how to make
Money
How to survive
I'm not stupid!
Know what I'm
Saying?
The people in the
Center
They been there too
They know how life
For us is
Some people just
Gotta do it
Some people do it
Just to do it
But some people
HAVE TO
A lot of people
Feel they have to
Dance topless bars to
Pay their way
Through college
Instead of asking
Mommy
For the tuition
Know what I'm
Saying?
Some kids do it
Because they
Hungry
They ain't got no
Money
Or their parents
They spending theirs
On drugs
They ain't got
Nothing else
To turn to
I mean
4.25 an hour
Ain't gonna get you
Nothing
Nothing!
$20 is nothing
These days
$20 AIN'T SHIT!

When I had a lot of boyfriends, I had two one night stands. I used a condom for both of them. Girl, I have so many condoms. (laughs) They stay in my house, so if I know I'm going out I have them. It was just with Ricky and Ben, that I didn't use them. Ben was my best friend. I knew his girlfriends, and he used to tell me everything. It wasn't like, I had to be so cautious. Me and Ricky were just friends. I knew some of his girls. He was, like, with this girl and that girl, on a rampage, doing things with a lot of girls. I told him, I knew how you was, and I chose to be with you. That's because I loved you. I don't hold what you done on you.

It's probably stupid
Not to think about
Using condoms with them
Even though you know a person
Like I thought I knew Ben
And he almost gave me a sexual disease
He used to have this thing on his penis
And I used to always tell him
Go to a doctor
Find out what that is
I was thinking it was
Just like a wart or something
He had syphilis
I flipped out
But I didn't catch it
I still trusted him
I don't know why

I have an apartment. It's my mother's apartment. The only ones who supposed to be in the house is me and my brother. But it's too crowded, because it's got my two stepsisters, my brother and my stepfather. There's three bedrooms. I choose to let them stay in there. I sleep in the living room. My stepfather's name is on the lease. I'm next of kin, but he's older than I am. It's my apartment, but as far as the management is concerned, he pays the rent. I could pay it. Welfare would give me 250 for it. But since he's the guardian of my brother, and he feels that he could handle it, be my guest.

My stepsisters are fifteen and nine. The fifteen year old says I'm selfish cause I don't clean up! Why should I clean if I don't have keys to my apartment? I don't have my own room. I gave up my room for y'all to live in. You not supposed to be here. So if anything, I can go down to the management and say, he has his kids living there. I'm pregnant, and I sleep in the living room. You'd have to leave.

And where you all gonna go?

With your mother? (archly)
The mother is a
Crack-head
Cocaine
Drunk-head
I know how it feels to be young
And have a parent who's
No good
I wouldn't want to be around
An adult who uses drugs and
Leaves you home two and three days
Cause she's out drinking
Or doing whatever she's doing
Y'all would be in the street with her
Looking all bummy
Hungry all the time

My stepfather told me don't leave. And I try to explain it. I have to leave. I cannot live in a place with so many people. I been around this neighborhood too long. I'm an adult now. I'm growing up. So life has to change. My surroundings have to change. Not the surrounders, because, people, everywhere you go, they have something wrong with their life. My baby's father, Ben got arrested last Saturday. (sucks her teeth) He broke a cop's wrist. Spit in his face. What ever possessed him? But then he's that type, like he doesn't care, authority or not. He won't do what he don't want to do. He don't talk about his problems. He doesn't feel that he could let them out. But yet he doesn't act like he got problems. He doesn't go around and beat. He'll laugh. Giggle. Cover up the pain. But some people just be, if they mad, they're gonna show they're mad. So stay out of my damn way! I mean, to a certain point, I'm like that.

Ben and me, we used to fight. He makes me look like a shrimp, but I would not care! We could be in the street or up here in the Center. He'd hit me, I'd hit him right back. I know that he could beat me up, but I didn't care. When I was mad I'd cry, and I'd just go up to him and hit him, start pulling his hair, knowing he could beat me up. Then you hear Sarah, the lady who runs the Center, coming downstairs, screaming, "You're at it again! Why can't you ever stop fighting? You kids are too much! Y'all stressing me out!"

I was living at the Center since I was 14. Sarah used to give us money to go to the movies. She never hit us. She never asked us to do anything, just basically go to school. That's all she used to tell us to do. And the meetings were sometimes cool. I went to the one for kids, Addicted Teens Anonymous. We made our group and the 12 steps. In the summer, if she saw you outside at 4 o'clock in the morning, she'd call in the cops, to get you off the block. That was when she used to throw us out.

When I left Sarah didn't know I was pregnant. We had got into a fight over the stove. Sarah has this rule that we can't be downstairs in the hotline. But I didn't care! I was hungry. So I went downstairs, and I was cooking in the kitchen. She told me to leave the kitchen. But, I'm pregnant, I'm hungry. I'm not gonna. So I told her no! I'm gonna finish this. (serious voice) "Well, if you don't obey my rules you're gonna have to leave, and find somewhere else." So I took that as, sort of fuck you too. I ate and then I left. Fuck you. You know what I'm saying? But I didn't want to tell her I was pregnant. Cause then, (mock serious) "Well, what you gonna do Maria?" She would try to convince me not to have the baby. I didn't want to hear nothing.

I could come back, but I don't want to live here. Sarah says it's fine, because there's people around here who are sober and clean. But I don't see it that way.

I see it as how I plan it

I have a baby

I have my own apartment

And it's me and my baby.

Not with a million people coming in and out of this building. Rats, cats, dogs! That's not how you raise a baby.

Until I get an apartment I'm just gonna have to settle, living with my stepfather. This is for time being, until I can do something for my kid. Now I'm just going to classes. I haven't been in two weeks. I feel tired. But I'm trying to get my GED. If I can't have my apartment and feel good about that, then I might as well have my GED (sweetly) and feel good about that. At least I'll have something, to show my kid. So I'm gonna be proud. Before I was pregnant I was just procrastinating. Just hanging out. You know, fuck it. What the heck. And now, I have to make some kind of change.

Maria's Themes

"I Have So Much Anger That I'm Ready to Just Hurt Anybody."

"When I'm mad, the best thing to do is stay away from me, cause I will hurt you. I don't care."

A prominent theme for Maria is her anger. Anger was evident in her manner during our interviews as she discussed various aspects of her life and her relationship with her mother. I noticed that she became much more animated when she expressed anger, as if energized by it. It seemed to be easier for Maria to express anger than sorrow. Although she told me about many sad experiences, she expressed sad feelings only once in the interviews, when she told me how her mother punched and kicked her when she was high. Even then I noted that her hurt was mixed with a good deal of indignation and anger. Her description of how she reacted to her father's death by "flipping" illustrated her belligerent style of dealing with painful events.

Maria talked about a number of things that aroused her anger. Her mother's denial of the possibility that she had AIDS, despite all the evidence pointing to the probability that she did, infuriated her. She told me she tried repeatedly to discuss her mother's HIV status with her, only to be rebuffed each time. Her mother's refusal to acknowledge what to Maria was obvious prevented their reconciliation and served only to increase Maria's rage. "She just couldn't do it. And the more she couldn't do it, the more I couldn't take it."

Her family's continuing denial of her mother's AIDS, especially their refusal to tell her younger brother about her history of drug abuse also angered Maria. There was a sense of righteousness and integrity in her insistence on disclosing the whole truth to him, and the way she described telling him, almost normalizing her mother's drug use, was even somewhat comforting. But there seemed to be a more hurtful aspect to her insistence that her brother know all. She wanted him told, "the way y'all told me", not shielding him from the full force of the truth. I thought that perhaps she wanted her brother to feel hurt, as she did.

One way Maria dealt with her anger was by "flipping", externalizing her anger through physical fighting or destroying her surroundings. She reacted to her father's death with a destructive rampage at school and at her grandmother's house. She also told me that she took out her anger by fighting with people. Although she said in our first interview that she wanted to stop fighting because it could be harmful for her baby, she missed an appointment for our second interview because she went to beat up a girl she'd had a disagreement with. She was eight months pregnant at the time.

Maria also attacked those she was closest to. She admitted to me with some guilt how she abused her baby brother because she was jealous of him. Sometimes she took out her anger on her long time boyfriend Ben, even though she was not even angry at him. She described how she would physically attack him when she was upset at something else. Maria even directed physical violence against herself, and she told me how she beat on her stomach during her first pregnancy.

Another way that Maria dealt with her anger, less blatantly but equally destructively, was through drug use. She admitted to smoking marijuana while she was pregnant, even though she was aware that it was not good for her unborn baby. She was apologetic, but she felt, "I have to," because she considered it an alternative to violence.

Maria expressed her anger with aggression and oppositionalism which were manifest in dangerous and illegal activities, such as drug use, destructiveness and assault. However, there were also benefits to her anger. Maria's fierceness made her appear strong and probably made her feel strong as well. Her propensity for physical violence must have been adaptive on the street, where her ferocity made potential aggressors back off. Her toughness and readiness to fight may have caused some fights, but they also may have protected her by making her difficult to victimize.

Ironically, her anger at her mother, which led to their estrangement, might also have provided an intimate form of connection. Maria identified with her mother in her extreme anger and violent way of acting it out. She told me, "I was just like her. I have so much anger that I'm ready to just hurt anybody." The anger that impeded their communication also served to connect them on a deeper level. Maria's fierceness and aggression also appeared to mobilize her and perhaps kept her from experiencing sadness at her many losses and deprivation and from sinking into despair.

"I Don't Want to Hear Nothing."

"Don't try to tell me what to do, cause I'm not having it. I do what I choose. If I want to do something I will. If I don't, nobody can make me."

Maria was ferocious in her assertion of her independence. She ignored rules when they conflicted with her own needs and desires and rejected help if she felt her independence might be compromised. When confronted with a problem she tended to defiantly defend her position rather than seek to resolve it. Sometimes she chose to withdraw from a situation rather than work things out. When I first met her she told me she was leaving New York because of troubles with her boyfriend. "I want to get away. I'd rather not deal with it. I rather just leave it alone."

Maria left the Center early in her pregnancy because she broke a rule by being in the kitchen and defied Sarah when confronted, rather than confiding in her and trying to work out the situation. "I didn't care! I'm pregnant, I'm hungry. So I told her no!" When Sarah told her she would have to obey the rules or find somewhere else to live Maria did not explain that she was hungry because she was pregnant, partly because she was offended and provoked by Sarah's ultimatum, and partly because she did not want to be told what to do. " I took that as, sort of fuck you too. I ate and then I left. Fuck you. But I didn't tell her I was pregnant, cause then she would try to convince me not to have the baby. I didn't want to hear nothing."

It seemed to be vital to Maria to feel that she was in control of her life. For the most part she refused to see herself as a victim and was defiantly self-sufficient. Her fiercely bristling stance of independence made it difficult for her to talk over problems and consider alternatives to her chosen course of action, and it alienated those who might help her.

Maria could also be oppositional and do things, not out of need, but out of anger, precisely because she was told not to. She was particularly galled by what she saw as her mother's hypocrisy in not practicing what she preached, telling her not to use drugs when she had done so for many years. Her mother's injunction not to use drugs provoked her oppositionalism to the point where Maria proclaimed that she would use drugs, even though she said that she didn't really want to when I questioned her about it.

"Nobody Wants to Be There to Help Me, The Hell with You!"

"I don't care if nobody wants to help me. I'm not asking for nothing! I can make it by myself."

Maria's sense that she was alone and would not receive support contributed to her anger. Rather than appear a pathetic, dependent and disappointed victim, she defiantly declared that she didn't need anything from anyone anyway. She made sure to emphasize that she didn't care if anyone helped her, because she could do for herself. She made a virtue out of necessity, flaunting her toughness, self-reliance and street savvy and suggesting that her lack of parental support had actually made her stronger and more mature.

> I've been in the streets since I was twelve. I've done a lot of things to support myself, like sell drugs. I know street life. You've had you mother there to buy you things and pat you on your back and wash your ass. I didn't have any parents to do that. So I know what it's like to be responsible.

Self-reliance meant the ability to survive, by any means necessary. She was contemptuous of those who were supported by their families, as well as of minimum wage jobs. "I mean, 4.25 an hour ain't gonna get you nothing. Nothing!" She felt she could do better selling drugs on the street.

Maria was ambivalent about getting support from her baby's father. She didn't expect to receive any because, "That's men's way of life. Ninety percent of men leave their children." She reacted to this belief with her typically fierce stance that she didn't need anything and could do it all by herself anyway. When Ben offered support she rejected him. "The baby doesn't need nothing. I don't want nothing from you." However, when pressed, she stated, "If I desperately needed it, because if the baby's his, he should have to do for it. If I choose for him to," being careful to establish herself firmly in control and dependent on no one.

"Some People Just Have To."

"I know drugs are bad, but sometimes I have to use them. Otherwise I'll be flipping. And I only deal drugs because I have to survive."

Although Maria said she hated her mother for using drugs, she nonetheless was involved with them herself as both a user and a dealer. She attributed both these activities to necessity. This was a sharp contrast to her frequent reference to the idea of choice and her stance of being in control. She saw many actions as choices, and at one point even described her drug use with some defiance as a choice. "I have a choice with smoking pot. I choose to do it, cause I want to! It's there, and I'll do it."

But Maria also framed her involvement with drugs in a more deterministic light, as when she described her drug use as a kind of self medication to prevent her violent behavior. "I guess I smoke when I feel like I can't take it. I'm always sorry. But sometimes I feel I have to! I'm that type. When I get really frustrated, down and out, I go and flip on somebody. Anybody."

Besides using drugs, Maria also sold drugs at times. Even though she knew that dealing was wrong, she felt that the deprivation and mistreatment she had suffered gave her no other options, and she should not be judged the same way as those who had had the support of their families. Unlike those kids who sold drugs, "just to do it" her motivation of survival justified her actions. "Some people do it, just to do it. But some people have to. Because they hungry, and they ain't got no money. They ain't got nothing else to turn to."

Maria recognized that her baby would place new demands on her for money, and she wondered whether she would have to risk selling drugs again to provide for the baby. "It makes it even harder cause I have to take care of the baby somehow. Welfare don't give you a lot. Should I just risk it, and, my kid will have? Or, just let my kid do without?"

Maria seemed to regard drug use in general as a given, a fact of everyday life. She explained her mother's drug use to her brother and made it seem almost normal, describing generational variations in the drug of choice almost like fashions in clothing.

In spite of this matter of fact attitude, there was still a covert aspect to drug use. Maria told me she never saw drug use or sales when her parents were active heroin users and dealers in their apartment. She initially denied her own current drug use, then admitted to occasionally smoking marijuana "blunts". Her initial denial and her statement that she apologized to her unborn child whenever she smoked indicated that she felt some guilt about her drug use.

"I Want to Have Something There, Cause I'm Here by Myself."

"My mother wanted me to have this baby. Because she ain't here to help me."

Her mother's death left Maria feeling very alone. She did not feel close to her surviving family and didn't get along well with them. The idea of having a baby gave her another chance to have a family. "It's not like my parents, but, just to have something there. The baby, that's your mother being with you, or, your father. Cause that's family."

From the very beginning of her pregnancy Maria realized that caring for a baby would be especially difficult for her. "I used to think, I can't have this baby, because I have no patience. I won't be able to handle it." She knew she was at risk to abuse the child because of her own history, but she felt she wouldn't.

> I know when people get smacked around they can end up smacking their own kids. But when you know it's yours, you treat it different. That's being cherished, not slapped around and starved. If I ever can't control myself, I can't say, cause I let it boil up before I hit. I stop myself a lot of times before I keep hitting. Believe me, I stop myself.

Although her mother had been adamant about not wanting her to have a baby, and in fact became enraged at her first pregnancy, after her mother's death Maria decided that her dead mother wanted her to have this baby. "She's the one that told me to have my baby." Her pregnancy provided Maria with a connection with her dead parents. When she agonized over whether she could cope with a child she felt her deceased parents' presence. "Somebody was over my shoulder. My father. My mother. Probably them both." She experienced this spiritual reunion as comforting and reassuring and interpreted it as a sign that she should go through with the pregnancy. When she failed to get an abortion she attributed this to their intervention.

Maria saw the baby quite literally as a replacement for her deceased parents, especially her mother. "Now that my mother's not here, she wanted me to have this baby . . . to replace her." She hoped that the baby would be a girl to replace her mother and planned to name her after her mother.

The baby was both a connection to her dead parents and the past and the embodiment of Maria's hope for the future. It would enable her to start over with a new family, one that would be closer to her and would revolve around her. Maria saw in motherhood a chance to change her life. "Maybe having a baby will change something. It will be something to help me change my life."

"It's Not Like I Have to Be So Cautious."

> I use condoms when I have a one night stand, but when I feel close to someone it's not like I have to be so cautious. I knew Ricky used to be doing things with

a lot of girls. But I chose to be with him. I love him. I guess I could still catch something, but I trust him.

Maria's love life was rather complicated and tumultuous. When it came to safer sex, she used condoms with partners she didn't know well, but she did not use condoms with either of her two steady boyfriends, even though she knew they both had other partners. Her feeling about Ben, with whom she had a close friendship as well as a love relationship, was that she knew him and his other girlfriends so well that there was no risk. Even after she narrowly missed contracting syphilis from him she still did not use condoms. While she was able to muse on the irrationality of her decision, "It's probably stupid not to think about using condoms," she did not change her behavior.

The question of whether or not to use condoms was an issue of trust for Maria. She did not base her decision on an assessment of risks. Instead it depended on her emotional attachment to her partner. If she felt love for the man she was with, she did not use condoms, regardless of what she knew of his sexual history or his other current partners. The fact that her mother had died of AIDS did not appear to enter into her decision of whether to practice safer sex.

"Doesn't Matter What You Do or Where You Go. Ain't Nothing Gonna Change."

"People everywhere you go, have something wrong in their life."

Behind her energizing anger and self medication with marijuana, Maria struck me as being depressed in her outlook on life, which was basically quite bleak and pessimistic. There was no hope for a better life. She felt that even efforts at change could wind up hurting. She attributed her mother's death, not to AIDS, but to stress brought on by her attempts at reform. "My mother wasn't sick when she died. She died from stress. She tried to change her whole life around and make up for what she did. It killed her."

She was troubled by the fact that she saw many people who had AIDS who continued to abuse drugs but were still alive. She told me about the mother of a friend from the neighborhood.

She don't wanna live, cause she's still choosing to use drugs. Then why is she still walking? For that God should take her away. 80% of the time it works that way. The drug addict lives. And those people who quit drugs died. Drugs. They say drugs kill you. I think drugs keep you alive."

Life was basically unfair. People who changed their lives died, while those who persisted in wrongdoing lived. Her perception was that this was the rule rather than the exception. It was not worth trying to change. You suffered and died anyway.

Maria declared herself an atheist, but it seemed to me that her atheism was not so much a disbelief in God as a disbelief in hope. She had a sense of "God" but felt He must be unfair. She briefly became angry when I asked her about her beliefs, then allowed quietly that, although she doubted that there was a God, "Maybe I want it to be." She wanted God to impose a sense of justice in the world, to punish wrongdoers and reward the good. However her perception of what was happening around her weighed heavily against this. There seemed to her no justice in who lived or died. It was futile to hope. Apart from any considerations of God, Maria had a spiritual side, as in her experience of her deceased parents' presence and their influence in guiding her to keep her baby.

Maria wanted to move, to escape the neighborhood she had known all her life and the troubled relationships she had there, especially with her boyfriends. However, she did not expect things would be much different elsewhere. " People everywhere you go, have something wrong in their life."

Maria's one possibility for hope was her baby. The baby would give her a reason to change her life and would keep her from being all alone in the world. In a rather insular but comforting vision of her future she declared, "I see it as how I plan it. I have a baby. I have my own apartment. And it's me and my baby."

TINA

I have known Tina for the past 6 years, as her counselor at school, as a confidant after her graduation, and most recently as an interviewer for this study. Our relationship continues to this day, and she calls me periodically "just to say hi" and to talk about what's going on in her life.

Because of our original counseling relationship, I did not approach her about participating in this study until six months after her graduation, when she had called me several times following the death of her mother from AIDS. I referred her to an agency for counseling then wrestled with the question of whether it would be a conflict of roles for me to invite her to participate in the study. I decided it would be acceptable, since our formal counseling relationship had ended, and she wanted to talk to me even after I had referred her elsewhere for counseling.

The interview arrangement met both of our needs. Because teens in AIDS affected families tend to move around a great deal, I had been having difficulty getting participants outside of my counseling practice who were accessible over time for follow up interviews. Tina wanted to do the interviews because of the familiarity and trust that we had built up when we worked together at school.

She also liked the idea of anonymously telling her story and possibly helping other teenagers who were going through similar experiences.

I want to introduce Tina as I came to know her in the two years I worked with her at our school and then to let her speak for herself through the material from our interviews. The chronology of her story can be confusing, both because Tina sometimes speaks of past events in the present tense, and because my privileged relationship with her gave me access to history which was not explicitly discussed in our interviews.

11/90:	Tina's father is murdered. She is 15 years old.
5/92–6/92:	I meet Tina and become her counselor for a short time
12/92:	Tina's aunt tells her that her mother has AIDS
2/93:	Tina unwillingly undergoes an abortion
3/93:	Tina attempts suicide. We resume our counseling relationship
7/93:	Tina becomes pregnant again
4/94:	Tina's daughter Danisha is born
6/94:	Tina's graduation. Our formal counseling relationship ends
11/94:	Tina's mother dies
5/95:	Tina's first interview with me
11/95:	Tina's second interview
2/96:	Tina's final interview
3/96:	Participant check with Tina. The next day Tina leaves for San Diego

I first met Tina in May of 1992 at a high school special education program for teenagers who were designated by the Board of Education as learning disabled. The Assistant Principal brought her to me for counseling because she had been living away from home and was involved in several exploitative and abusive relationships with male students. The AP was concerned about her extremely erratic attendance and felt she was at risk for contracting a sexually transmitted disease or HIV.

Tina was a petite, small-boned young African-American woman with clear, cafe-au-lait skin and lush, full lips. She wore her black hair slicked back into a bun or straightened and arranged in the latest styles. She was always beautifully coiffed, and her clothes, while not expensive, were often new and carefully coordinated. She had a sweet, unassuming demeanor which was very endearing and immediately evoked in me a desire to protect her. She connected easily with me and said that she had wanted a woman counselor so she could talk openly.

Up close I realized that, although her face was invariably clean and subtly made-up, her hygiene was inconsistent, and she sometimes smelled like she had not had a bath recently. I noticed the slight clumsiness of her hands and the fact that she had to hold papers close to her face in order to read them. She was in fact legally blind in her left eye and impaired in her right. However, she was loath to admit that she needed glasses, and she never wore them.

Tina's sweet, friendly manner belied her statement to me that she didn't like most people and didn't want to get close to anyone. By her own account she had a quick temper and a sharp tongue and in the past had been involved in frequent arguments with other students. Despite her small stature, these fights sometimes became physical, even with much larger and stronger opponents.

Tina seemed unselfconsciously proud of her natural beauty and received the attentions of male admirers with quiet pleasure. Keeping a steady man was much harder. In our first session she seemed to derive great pleasure in detailing the attributes of her newest beau, telling me of their plans to marry as soon as he left the army. Her attendance was erratic, so it was two weeks until our next meeting. By that time the young man she had described was no longer in her life. She told me about another beau at school, with whom she had previously lived. She had chased him in the street with a knife because he was seeing another girl. She said she didn't care about him any more because she was happy with her new man. When I asked her new man's name she couldn't remember it.

She soon began to tell me about her family. She talked about her father and how his murder three years earlier had devastated her. She also talked about her fights with her mother, describing how her mother had thrown her out of the house yet again and put her clothing out on the fire escape. She said she and her mother had never gotten along. From the time she was 15 years old she had lived with various friends, moving from house to house as her welcome wore out. She stayed only sporadically with her mother and usually left because of fierce fighting between them. She was vague about the cause of their arguments, but she told me that some of the problems had to do with her refusal to accept her mother's rules.

Tina and I only met a few times that Spring before school ended in late June. In September she was sent to a distant work/study site and re-assigned to a counselor there. I didn't hear much about her until March, when I received a frantic phone call from the Assistant Principal, who told me that Tina had tried to kill herself by taking an overdose of pills and had just been released from the hospital. She asked me to resume counseling with her. When I met with Tina later that day we discussed some of the issues which had led to her suicide attempt, including a recent abortion which she had undergone unwillingly. Her former boyfriend, the father of the unborn child, had been so enraged at her plan to continue the pregnancy that he had physically assaulted her in the street. Her mother also insisted on the abortion. She sorrowfully told me that, while she felt it was true that, "I wouldn't be able to be a good mother, at least I could've tried." For several weeks prior to her suicide attempt, Tina had been living with her friend Marisol's family. Tina spoke of the close relationship Marisol had with her mother and how it saddened her to compare it to her relationship with her own mother.

Tina still visited her mother from time to time, but she was adamant about their inability to live together. This left her with no reliable family to support her and no source of income. Survival was a big issue for her. I proposed that we work to make her an "independent woman" by finding a source of income and housing of her own. When I learned that Tina's mother was collecting Welfare benefits for her I offered to help her to open her own case. Tina refused, saying, "I don't want to mess my mother up." I suggested applying for Supplemental Security Income (SSI). She told me they had turned her down in the past. However, when I explored this with the agency, they told me her application had been denied because she did not keep appointments for interviews. She applied again, and because of her learning disability and visual impairment she qualified.

Finding housing was far more difficult. I helped her to apply for supported housing, but there was a long wait. In the meantime, Tina continued to live in Marisol's overcrowded household, where ten people shared three bedrooms. Tina slept in Marisol's room, at first sharing a mattress on the floor with Marisol's teenaged brother, Luis. Marisol's mother approved of the relationship, saying that Tina was "for Luis". However, when Ramon, a younger but more aggressive brother returned to the house in April he supplanted Luis. By the summer Tina was pregnant, as, coincidently, were Marisol and two of her sisters. Ramon very quickly moved on to other girlfriends. Tina told me that he asked her to iron his clothes before dates. She decided to continue the pregnancy, with the support and blessing of Marisol's family. She felt a sense of unity with the three other pregnant young women in the household. She told me how she enjoyed going to prenatal clinic visits with the sisters and planning for their babies, who would be cousins.

Marisol's family was deeply involved in the drug trade of their South Bronx neighborhood, which caused a great deal of violent upheaval for them during the time Tina lived with them. That summer Marisol's mother's boyfriend, a drug user, stole drugs from local dealers, leading to threats of murder against him and everyone else in the house. These were not idle threats. Just two months earlier Marisol had been the first one to discover the body of her twenty year old neighbor and a friend stabbed to death in their apartment down the hall.

No sooner did this scare subside when other drug related violence threatened the household. Ramon and Luis were dealing drugs when Ramon shot and seriously wounded another dealer. The two brothers fled out of state, but once again the rest of the household feared being killed in retribution. Fortunately for Tina, our efforts at finding alternate housing bore fruit, ironically because her pregnancy had moved her to the top of the waiting list. That fall she returned to her mother's apartment for a few months and then moved into a supported apartment.

During this time Tina and I continued our therapeutic work. Once she felt her practical needs were being addressed I tried to focus more on emotional issues. It was then Tina confided in me that her mother had AIDS.

Tina's Story

My mother always said that I was the stubborn one out of everybody. Which is true, cause you can't tell me nothing and don't think I'm not gonna tell you nothing back. I'm like her, cause she got her stubborn ways too. Whatever she said, I always did the opposite, or I always gave her backtalk about it. When she was sick I told her, I don't want to get close to you because I know I'm gonna lose you soon. So I'd rather just stay apart. I thought it would be easier on me. But I see now that it's not. I see that it's just harder on me. I didn't get close. But it still hurted.

You would never think my mother would get AIDS. She was not a person that used to party. That lady, even on nice days, she would stay in the house. She'd never go outside hardly. It would have to be like, real, real hot for her to go outside. Or else she got to be real bored in the house. She was never the type that used to talk. She would only say hi and bye to you. That was it. But as to conversating with you, she wasn't all in to that. She was like the quiet type.

I don't know how she got AIDS. I don't know if she shot drugs. That part she never told me. But that's all that I could think of. Cause my mother was never involved with nobody after her and my father separated. So the only thing I can think of is drugs.

My mother didn't tell me that she was sick for a long time. She told my two sisters first. I don't know who I was living with then. I know I wasn't home. I didn't know until my aunt told me.

I DIDN'T KNOW NOTHING.

Tina's twelve-year-old sister Melissa is sitting on the living room couch watching tv. Her mother is sitting quietly on a chair nearby. Suddenly the mother stands up.

Mother: "No!"

Melissa: "Mom, what's the matter? Why'd you say that?"

Mother: "I got it."

Melissa: "You got what?"

Mother: "I got the virus. The AIDS virus."

Melissa begins to cry and walks over to her mother and hugs her.

Melissa: "Don't worry Mom, everything's gonna be ok. (pauses) We gotta tell Lashawn when she gets home. And what about Tina?"

Mother: "I don't know. I just don't know."

The two cry quietly, embracing in the middle of the living room.

TINA DISCLOSURE

It was a couple days before Christmas. My aunt said, "Tina, you know what your mother got?" And I was like, "What?" And she was like, "She got what I got." And I said, "What you mean?" But when she said that, I automatically knew, cause my mother told me about her.

We had brung it up somehow, I don't re-member. My mother said, "Auntie is sick. She got the AIDS virus." My heart just dropped. I didn't even know how to act when my aunt walked back in the house, cause she was staying with us for a couple of days. My mother said, "Don't say nothing. Let her tell you. Cause she might not want you to know." And I was like, "Ok, I'm not gonna say nothing."

I took it calmly, cause I didn't want to look suspicious. I waited til my aunt told me she had the virus. Then I said I didn't know. She said, "You didn't know I had it?" I didn't want to say yeah, cause my mother said don't say nothing. So I said, "No, I didn't know." She said, "I thought they told you." I said, "Auntie, when it comes down, you know nobody tells me nothing.

I DIDN'T KNOW NOTHING."

So, I knew about my mother, but I didn't bring it up until I was pregnant with Danisha. She never said anything to me about herself, cause she didn't know how to tell me. My mother and me, we didn't talk. But when I was pregnant with Danisha I felt like, it's better for me to try to get the tightness with my mother now.

Me and my sisters was in the kitchen, and my mother was coming back from somewhere. As she was walking in the door, I said to my sister, "Do you know about Mommy? Do you know about our mother got AIDS?" She say yeah. And my mother say yeah. But I didn't say anything else about it until my mother told me first. Then I told her that I didn't know. Again. Like I told my aunt.

I DIDN'T KNOW NOTHING.

And then we talked about, am I gonna be alright when she leaves. I told her yeah.

Me and my mother started getting close, after I had Danisha. That's her first granddaughter that she ever had. Everything change when she got to that hospital and seen her! When she seen her, she was all happy. It changed her. Cause she got to see her granddaughter before she left. She got to see one of her kids have a kid. It meant a lot to her. Even though she thought I wasn't gonna be ready. I just thank God that she got to see Danisha. She got to hold her.

I look at Danisha and
I think about that saying
They say God will always give a life
Before He takes a life
He gave me Danisha in replace of my mother
And I believe that
Because
When my father passed five years ago
Is when I got pregnant the first time
I thought He gave me a life for a life
I always believe that saying
That God never close the door
Without opening up a window
God takes a life
He give you a life
So
I always say
God knew He was gonna take my mother soon
So he gave Danisha in return

It took for Danisha to be born. That's when my mother started getting a little bit sicker. That's probably why she didn't really want to stay. Cause she was getting attached to Danisha. But then again she was like kinda staying her distance from Danisha cause she knew she was leaving soon. She might've thought it made it easier.

It makes it harder for me, because the things that Danisha do, I be wanting to go back to her. Like when she first started walking, I wanted my mother to see her first steps. When she starts talking I want my mother to see. I be wanting to call up and be like, "Ma, Danisha did this! Ma, Danisha did that!" And then I be catching myself and be like, (softly) she's not there.

Before she died I was worried about, if, God forbid, she would've passed in the house, while we was there. Or when we woke up one morning she didn't wake up. That's all I thought about. So in a way, God let it happen with her in the hospital, instead of her at home. It would've been much harder for us at home. All I thought about was my little sister, cause she slept with my mother sometimes. What about if she woke up one day, and my mother don't wake up?

Or when me and my older sister moved out again, I always used to be scared too about, what if my little sister come home one day, and my mother is gone. And she had to walk in the house and see that. But God let her pass in the hospital. So in a way that's kinda good. Because, at least she was around doctors and everything. When she did go, it was always somebody around her.

When she went to the hospital the last time, they told us that she was getting real, real sick, and they don't know if she's gonna be released anytime soon. Then the doctor had told us that we had to sign the paper stating, when the machine stop that we didn't want them to save her. We didn't want them to poke at her. Nothing, just leave her. Cause that's what my mother always said. If she had to pass in the hospital, she didn't want nobody to save her. She wanted just to go. So, we signed the paper. It was hard because, that's when we really, really knew that she had gone. That the machine was only keeping her there, and it was just a matter of hours before that machine stopped.

My older sister was at the hospital, and all my aunts were there. The doctor came out and told us that we should go in there and say goodbye to her because she only had one hour to live. It was less than an hour. When my mother passed, it was only 15 minutes after the time that the doctor was telling them.
I felt it when my mother passed
I always say God kept me from it
Cause I was supposed to go see my mother that day
I was heading up to see her
I don't know
My sister called me
And I was saying
I'm coming
I'm coming
And then
I didn't get nowhere!
It was like
I stood there still
I didn't know what for
I knew nothing
It was just something keeping me there
Sometimes I be scared
Cause a lot of things that happen
I can feel them before they happen
That's scary in a way
I felt my mother going
It was something
Keeping me in my house

Saying
Don't go
And I just
Didn't go.
The phone rang at 12 o'clock
And I automatically knew
Something just told me
I picked it up and started crying
I said you don't have to tell me
Cause I already had felt it
Mommy had just passed

That's like when my father died. When the phone rang, I jumped up. I knew. I didn't even have to hear it or wait 'til my mother cry. I already knew. My father died when I was 15 years old. He died cause of mistaken identity. After my father got out of jail, he didn't live with us, but he was coming down to see us for Thanksgiving. My mother and my father's sister was sending him his money to come down, and he was going to the post office to get it. On his way there, a guy shot him from the back. When they turned him over, it was mistaken identity.

My mother said that it was better if I didn't go to his funeral, because of the way I would take it. She said, don't get mad at her, she's just doing what's best for me. So I ended up not going. At first I wanted to go, but now I think about it and I'm glad I didn't go. Cause they would have to bury me with him. So, it was the best thing for me not to go.

When my father passed, at first I didn't want to accept it. To this day I still don't. I guess it's true. I don't know. I just don't feel like he's gone. If I was to go to the funeral and see him, I think I would feel like he's gone. But I don't. My mother, I know she's gone. Inside I don't accept it, but how I know she's gone, cause I seen her. When my father passed, I was always feeling like he was here. That's not how I feel with my mother. I don't be expecting her. I mean, I'm wishing that she'd walk through the door, but I know that she's not going to. I don't know. To me, whether you see them or not, you still don't accept that they gone.

I went to my mother's funeral. It was ok, up until it was time to leave, and we had to put the flowers on. When it was time for me to go up there my uncle had to hold Danisha and hold me. I put my flower on, and then I held the casket, and I kissed her. I said, "Danisha's gonna miss you, and she's gonna love you. And I always love you." And I kissed the casket. On my way walking back to the limousine I came back to my mother's casket, and I was like, "No, don't take her!. Don't take her!" My sister started crying, and she said, "Leave her." My uncle said, "Just let it all come out." Then my uncle took me and said, "Tina, it's time to go. You gotta go."

I cried for my mother the whole ways back to my grandmother's. Then I wiped my eyes off and got out the limousine. My older sister hugged me. I said, "I'm sorry for the scene I made." She said, "No, it's gonna always be harder for you because you never had that close relationship with Mommy, like we did."

They're gonna get together and put a stone on where she's at. It's gonna say her full name and the day she was born, up until the day she passed (softly). They've been there once. They wanted me to go, but I told them I didn't want to go. I ain't ready to go yet. I got to get my mind together first before I could be able to go anywhere. Part of me is saying that it's time for me to realize that she's gone. But it's harder for me because, with my mother, we didn't have that, close relationship that mothers and daughters have. I never really sat and talked to her. I never told her, like, what was bothering me. I don't talk to none of my family. So they don't know how I feel inside, they don't know what I'm thinking. I don't talk to nobody. That's me. I'm just a cold person. It takes a lot to get something out of me.

My sisters are dealing with it. Except for my older sister. She's really starting to lose it now. It's really starting to bother her. My sisters are leaving me in a few months. They're going to Georgia. Our intention wasn't supposed to be to split up. Our intention was supposed to leave out of New York City. But I'm not ready to go that far.

I just want to just get away
And be by myself for awhile
I want to find myself
Because I'm so confused
I don't know what to do
I'd rather just go
And get myself together
I think then things will be a little bit easier for me
I don't know
At times I be wanting to pull my hair out
At times I be wanting to just
Go crazy
I don't know
I got to get control for Danisha

I'd rather Danisha call me by my name than call me Mom. Everybody tells me it's wrong for her to call me Tina, and I should get her out of that habit. But nobody understands that I'd rather her to be like that. I don't want Danisha to have the relationship me and my mother had. So I feel like, if she calls me Tina she'll feel closer to me, and it'll be easier to talk to me. But if she was like, "Oh

I got to tell my mother this. I ain't gonna be able to tell her!" she's gonna get mad at me. But if she know that I'm like a big sister to her, I'm the person she could come and talk to.

Danisha's the only one I got
If you take Danisha
I definitely don't have nothing
A man can always go
They can always walk
No matter what
But Danisha is
Right now
All I got
Now that my mother and father are gone
And my sisters are leaving me
And Danisha's father
I know what he's gonna do
So I say
Well
Danisha's my daughter
And she calls me Tina
And she says her little words to me
Like her baby talk
Or whatever
But
She's not a person I could sit and conversate with
It really bothers me
That she don't know no better
She's just a baby

I've been out of it lately. My head hasn't been with me. Like I don't remember nothing hardly no more. Like what did I do. Where did I put stuff at. I lost my wallet, with all my stuff in it. I used to always remember where I put stuff. Now I gotta think. (Sighs) It's like I'm losing all my memory. I guess cause it's starting to bother me more now.

Right after she passed it wasn't really bothering me that much. But, out of my family, I'm the one that keeps it in. Everybody else talks to each other. I keep my tears in. There's a lot that I still don't let out. And that's why I be feeling the way that I feel.

How do I feel?
I'm mad
I'm mad because
I don't know
I'm mad at my mother
I think the reason why
I don't feel bad
I mean
I feel bad
But the reason
I don't cry
A lot
Cause I think I'm angry
I know I'm angry
I'm angry
Because
My mother could've
Left
Any other way

TINA
STRESS

She could've left of
Old age
Anything else
But AIDS

My father, I miss him, and I talk about him still. He left, by somebody else's stupidity! Cause he got shot. When my mother left, I can't say it was through her, stupidity, or that.

I think about it and I be like, should I get mad at her, for leaving us? Sometimes I get mad, and sometimes I look at it and say, I don't know. I mean, it's not her fault. She didn't ask for AIDS. She didn't ask Him please give it to me. So. That's why I look at it like that and say, I'm not mad at her. I'm just mad cause she left. But it's not her fault that she left. Because, if my mother had a choice, she would've picked to stay.

Me and my mother, we didn't have a good relationship. I was always the type that don't tell nobody how I feel. I still am like that. But like, if I hit Danisha or if I yell at her, I'll hug her real quick, because I'll be concerned. Cause, I'm missing my mother a lot, and I took everything out on her.

In March 1993 Tina tried to kill herself with an overdose of pills. When I met with her after her release from the hospital, she told me with fierce bravado how she had refused an emetic in the emergency room and chose instead to have her stomach pumped, because it was riskier. Although she had been warned that moving while the stomach tube was in place could kill her, she told me how she had thrashed about, causing profuse bleeding and necessitating her being tied to the gurney.

When she removed her sunglasses I saw that the entire white of her right eye was an eerie dark red, the result of the physical trauma she had gone through. BASED ON MY COUNSELING NOTES 3/93

My aunt said I should let her know what's bothering me, because that's why I used to be as suicidal as I was. Because I used to always let things build up inside of me and never talk to nobody. And, she didn't want that to happen. I think about suicide from time to time. Only thing that I say to this day, and I thank God for it, is Danisha. If I go, where is she gonna be at? Is she gonna be ok and everything?

I'm ok. Kicking it. Taking it easy. (small sad laugh). With Danisha ain't nothing else to do but be alright. She stress me out from time to time. But, I can handle it. It's just, the week of my mother's going. This Sunday made a year for her. So since then, I was like moody towards Danisha. But that was natural, because it was almost a year since my mother passed.

Marisol always told me
Whenever somebody pass away
You can always light them a candle
And pray for them
And it will help you a lot
So
I bought a candle for my mother
I put her picture by it
I prayed for her
(Sigh)
And now I'm just taking it easy
It helped me
Cause
I light a candle up for the day that she passed
I light a candle up for Mother's Day for her
And I light a candle up for her birthday
So it's like three times
I light a candle up for her
When you light a candle
Even if you don't pray to that person
You can talk to that person
Even though that person can't talk back to you?
You'll feel better
Cause of a lot of things
You let off your chest

I been doing it ever since she been gone. I did it for her last week, then I called my sisters, and I made sure they was alright. My sister said yeah, and she asked me if I was alright. I told her, it's hard. I cried a little bit, but my mother wouldn't want us like that. Us three been being real strong. Being that it's the holidays, it's kind of hard for us.

But we handling it though
Taking it easy
Nothing else to do

My aunt with AIDS is real sick right now. Every time she's in the hospital, I never go see her. And there's gonna be a time that I'm not gonna see her and she's not gonna make it out. Then I'm gonna regret it. Like with my mother. I didn't want to go see her. Halloween I went to go see her, and she still wasn't talking, cause they had a lot of tubes in her. That was last time I seen my mother, on Halloween. Two days later is when she passed. (very quietly) I don't know. I feel like if I go see my aunt she gonna be the next one to pass. That's why I don't want to go see nobody. Cause with my mother, I just got that feeling that if I didn't go see her, maybe she'd still be here. And now with my aunt, I feel like I shouldn't go see her. But then again, something tells me, just go see her, and maybe you'll feel more better. I'ma just go and get it over with.

Cause, see, my aunt I can talk to, and if I don't feel right, I could just let her know and she don't get upset or nothing. She said that she would understand, cause she know what I just gone through with my mother. And she knows probably soon it's gonna be her turn. She's getting skinny, just like my mother was when she got into her last stage. My mother, she was always small, so when she lost weight, there was just nothing. And she getting dizzy and stuff, just like my mother. For some reason, I guess cause my mother told me about her first, I always got prepared to see her go before my mother. But, I feel like if I go see my aunt, she's gonna pass too. I rather don't go see her. I'll go see her, but I have to be like, real up to go see her.

It took a long time for me to say anything to you
About my mother having AIDS
Because it took a long time for me to
Accept
That she would be leaving me soon
My father was gone
And now my mother was gonna go
It took a lot out of me
And I had to understand
That when she go
God was only taking her
Instead of having her in pain and suffering
So I understood it like that
And then
From me taking classes and seeing tapes
It made me realize
That there's a lot of things that you can't get
From a person that has AIDS
And that when that person has it
That you gotta accept
That person gonna leave you
Might not leave you no time soon
But

You gotta accept
That they gonna go.

I only told one other person about my mother. This girl I knew for 10 years, who lived on my block. Her mother was like my mother. I can't get attached with everybody, but with her mother I just clicked. Her mother's another person I knew that passed before they told me. I don't like anybody to get close to me, cause I know when you're getting ready to go. But I knew her mother had AIDS, and I was like, well, I feel that I could talk to her now. So, we call each other time to time. I don't talk to her about it a lot. But, like when I feel like it's really bothering me, I let her know.

Everybody else
I told them that she passed of cancer
I always say it was cancer
Cancer
I always make sure that I don't never slip
Make sure it's cancer
If I slipped
I don't know
People think of AIDS like
Talking to a person you can get it
And I hate people like that
I be ready to knock them out
It's so many ignorant people like that
And it's not true!
I say that if everybody get AIDS by talking
By sitting where the person sat
Everybody here would have AIDS
It makes me mad
Like when I used to be in school
Then they used to talk about it
And they used to show a film
Just looking at the film
I used to just sit there
And just be like
You all so stupid!

Ramon is Danisha's father. Me and his sister Marisol been friends for a long time, and I was living with her family when I got pregnant from him. My mother knew that he was gonna walk and it was gonna be on me. She told me, "A man is gonna go." But I let her know, Ma, you took care of three of us by yourself. (hesitates)

My father came and was gone

He walked
In and out of our life
He was the type of father that promised something
But if he didn't give it
We didn't always be like
But you promised
More or less he was there
But he gave us his love
That was good enough for us.

That's how I feel about Ramon. Since Danisha's a year now, he never gave her nothing in her life. And she needed this and she needed that. And I tell him, I can always buy Danisha something, and it could be from you, and you give it to her. Danisha's small. She don't understand nothing right now. All she need is your love. She needs to spend more time with you. I don't talk bad about you to her. I got the two pictures that we took together. And I show Danisha that every other day, letting her know. That's your father. He's not here. He's out to the store. I'm always making excuses. I don't never talk bad about him.

It's hard
My money don't last
Danisha only get a little bit of money from Public Assistance
And I receive Social Security
But now that I got my own apartment
I'm paying bills
And
My money don't last
By the 10th of the month
I'm broke
I gotta make sure that Danisha got everything
And make sure that I got everything
Make sure that there's stuff that we need around the house
Like soap
And all that
I tell him to understand and just to help me out
Just a little bit
I'm not asking him to come into my life

I told him, I'm going always to be on you the way I'm on you. Because for the simple fact is I have a daughter, and I can't do it by myself. Because it's hard. I don't ask for nothing. I don't care how badly I need it, I don't ask you. And he said that's why he's like that with me. He don't never give me cause I don't never ask for it. I told him that I should never have to ask. You should be able to come and give it to me, without me asking.

I always have had low self esteem. I went through verbal abuse from Ramon, and I went through physical abuse from him. He hit me. He said that I was ugly and that I would never find nobody. The next man that I found was gonna dog me. Now I'm getting my esteem. I'm not taking that anymore. I talk back now, and he don't like it. He's used to the Tina that's quiet, that let him do what he want to do. Now I'm thinking for Danisha. I don't let nobody walk over me or nothing. I always have to be like that now, because, my mother and father are not here. So when something happens I can't run to them. The day that my mother passed, my attitude had changed. I used to let him walk all over me. But now I stand up to him. The moment that I let you walk over me, Danisha's gonna see it. She's gonna feel that, in order for a man to love you they have to hit you. And that's not true.

He's staying with some chick now (with great disdain). He ain't happy. That don't make me no difference, cause he's in a position that he want to be in. I don't let him know if stuff bothers me or not, and he don't like that. He wanted to take Danisha for the weekend, but he gotta know, he cannot. He living with her, and she could be a crackhead. I'm saying, since you're with her, then you can't get with Danisha, because I don't want her to be around drugs. I don't do it. If I do decide to smoke weed, I always make sure that Danisha's not around me, or she's sleeping.

He never thought I was gonna have an Order of Protection on him. I always said it and I never did it. The reason why I did it is cause the day when I brought Danisha out to see him, and you picked your girl at the time over Danisha. Where's that girl at now? She's not with you now. And Danisha will always be there for you.

Now that he got a job. Thank God, he coming around. He's trying to help me for Christmas for her. He called me the other day and asked me what does she need and everything. He can't bring it because of the Order of Protection I got on him. But he told me, whenever I drop it he'll come. So, he'll buy the stuff, little by little, for Danisha. And, by Christmas I should have 'em (sighs). I told him, well, keep it up. Because last year for Christmas I bought her everything. I told him, you don't always got to buy her nothing. Because when I can't buy her, I give her love. And you can't buy love. I'm gonna drop the Order of Protection, cause it would be best for Danisha. It's not because I love him. It's cause I'm thinking about Danisha.

I'm happy because, I met a new guy I'm with through my next door neighbor, Charise. Her man is locked up in jail, and my friend is locked up there too, for selling drugs. Me and him talk. We laugh, we joke. He understands me. He's got a daughter, two years old. He dropped his baby's mother because of me. He said that he's not worried, because I told him that I would be there for him. I told him I'd come see him every chance I get.

He tells everybody about me. Everytime I get on the phone everybody who know him is talking to me! They yelling in the background, "Hi, Tina!" And I be like, "Everybody know me!" We just got a good relationship. When I was on the phone with him Charise yelled "You got to see how she look! Cause she's smiling from ear to ear." And he said, "Tell her I'm the same way. Everytime I talk to you everybody here is yelling, 'Hey, you got to see the way he is on this phone with you!'" I told him to tell his friend to mind his business. He said, "Tina, I can't mind my business, cause when I want to go to sleep I can't, cause he want to sit up and talk to everybody about you."

Usually
When I meet somebody
I be like
Oh gosh
(sucks her teeth)
He's gonna be all on me.
And I ain't gonna try to get
Him the time of day

TINA
LOVE

But we just clicked
I feel like this is
The right one
After all I been through
I feel like God is just now
Finally sending me
The right one

He'll be leaving Riker's Island and going upstate for 7 months. He said that if I can stick it out with him, that will make him have more energy to hurry up and do the time. I told him, I'm doing time with him. Only thing is, I'm out here, and he in there. When he come out, he gonna get a job. He said, "Mami, I don't want to sell drugs. Because I know you don't like it." I told him (mock indignation) "No. Because what you gonna do for me, locked up?!"

He'll move uptown
So he can be closer to me
I would never have to
Worry
About needing nothing
He's always gonna give it
To me
Even now
If I need something
All I got to do is just tell him
He'll have somebody
Give it to me
I told him that's ok
I'm not like that
If I really do need
I feel like I'm gonna get it
I'm on Social Security
My check is enough

I didn't have enough
Money to
Pay my phone bill
And he said to me

"Hey Mami
When your phone
Get cut off
You know we can't talk to
Each other no more"
I said
"But there's pen & paper"
And he said
"You go girl!"
But yesterday made me
Realize
That it's hard
If I don't talk to him
I feel down
I started feeling sick
When I get depressed
I get sick
Like real bad headaches
And my stomach start
Hurting
And yesterday
I was OOOH!
I felt like it was the
End of the world
He stopped calling me

A week later the relationship ended when Tina paid a surprise visit to him in jail and found his former girlfriend, the mother of his daughter, there.

Not long after that, Tina began another telephone romance with the brother of a new friend. The brother, who lived in California invited her to move out to the West Coast to stay with him. She accepted, but since she couldn't afford plane fare she and two year old Danisha had to take a three day trans-continental bus trip. This was a very difficult trip for them both, but Tina was drawn by the hope of love and a new beginning and left with Danisha for California to live with a man she had never met. MY FIELD NOTES-APRIL, 1996

Tina's Themes

"Me and My Mother Didn't Have a Good Relationship."

Tina told me many times that she did not have a good relationship with her mother. Their problems getting along seemed to be a longstanding pattern, rather than a response to her mother's illness. Tina told me that from the time she was fifteen she had lived off and on with various friends because she did not get along with her mother. She returned home from time to time but always left after a few months because of fierce fighting.

Although Tina maintained that she did not want to get close to her mother, she also spoke several times about wanting to "get the tightness with her." Even though they fought a lot, Tina still craved her mother's attention. She had been deeply disappointed when her mother had told her she would not be at her graduation.

"My sister said she was gonna come. And my little sister too. I didn't mind them coming. But mostly I wanted my mother to come. That's the only main person I wanted to come, cause, you always want your mother to be there."

Despite her positive feelings, whenever Tina lived with her mother they resumed fighting and Tina left in anger. Tina never really explained to me why they fought so much, other than to say that she did not want to follow her mother's rules, such as curfews. Tina seemed to feel uncomfortable about expressing anger at her mother, especially in regard to AIDS. Right after telling me that she was mad at her mother for dying of AIDS, she said that she wasn't mad because it wasn't her mother's fault that she got AIDS. "That's why I look at it like that and say, I'm not mad at her."

Whatever their difficulties, Tina did not speak ill of her mother or talk to me about what had caused the rift between them. I suspected her mother's drug use might have been a problem, but Tina declined to talk about this. She never discussed her mother's drug problem with me, even though I asked her several times. When I asked Tina if she thought her mother had contracted HIV through intravenous drug use she told me,

> I don't know. I don't think, that part she never told me. But that's all that I could think of. Cause my mother was never involved with nobody after her and my father separated. So the only thing I can think of is drugs.

Even in admitting to the possibility of her mother's drug use, she seemed to be putting her in the best possible light by stressing her loyalty to Tina's absent father.

"I Don't Want to Get Close."

Tina was explicit about her desire to stay apart from her mother as a strategy for dealing with her impending loss. She said that she told her mother, "I don't want to get close to you because I know I'm gonna lose you soon. So I'd rather just stay apart."

This strategy of mitigating pain by not getting close had great resonance for Tina. She attributed the same philosophy to her mother. She felt her mother didn't want to get too attached to Danisha because she knew she was dying. Tina felt her mother's desire not to be hurt by an attachment to her granddaughter even precipitated her deteriorating medical condition soon after Danisha's birth.

> It took for Danisha to be born. That's when she started getting sicker. That's probably why she didn't really want to stay. Cause she was getting attached to Danisha. But then again she was kinda staying her distance from Danisha cause she knew she was leaving soon. She might have thought it made her easier.

But, as Tina found, distancing herself didn't help to avoid pain. "I didn't get close. But it still hurted though. I see that it's just harder on me."

"I Always Say It Was Cancer."

Tina did not want anyone to know that her mother died of AIDS. She felt that she had to conceal that fact, intimating that if people knew they might think that she was infected as well. Of all the things we spoke about in our interviews, this made her the most furious.

Within her family as well, AIDS was a difficult subject. Her mother did not tell her about her own infection. Instead she told her about her aunt, but cautioned her not to say anything. When her aunt assumed that Tina knew about her illness, Tina maintained that, "I didn't know nothing." After her aunt disclosed her mother's illness, Tina kept silent about it for several months. It wasn't until she felt closer to her mother during her pregnancy that she spoke with her about it. Even after she brought up the subject of her mother's AIDS, she maintained to her mother that she hadn't known.

This denial and secrecy around disclosure was reflected in Tina's relationship with me when I was her counselor. Even though she had unflinchingly shared many intimate details about her life with me, Tina said nothing about her mother's AIDS to me for several months after her mother disclosed to her that she had AIDS. When I asked her later if she would like to be in a group with other counselees who also had family members with AIDS she declined, saying she didn't want anyone, even other affected peers to know about her situation.

"My Baby Is All I Got."

Tina told me that her baby was all she had, and she meant many things for Tina. Danisha was a connection to her mother, a gift to her dying mother, a replacement for her, a reason to be strong, an accomplishment, and, she hoped, someone to love her.

First and foremost, Danisha's birth brought about a reconciliation between Tina and her mother. In spite of all her mother's misgivings about her ability to parent, Tina felt her baby was very meaningful to her mother. Danisha enabled Tina to draw closer to her mother near the end of her life.

> Me and my mother started getting close, after I had Danisha. That's her first granddaughter that she ever had. Everything change when she got to that hospital and seen her. She was all happy. Cause she got to see her granddaughter before she left. She got to see one of her kids have a kid. It meant a lot to her.

Tina was thankful that her mother got to see Danisha before she died. Danisha was Tina's gift to her mother, a reassurance even in the face of death that a part of her would live on. This struck me when I met Tina's mother at the school reception for Tina's graduation. She was extremely thin and frail, but Tina had left two and a half month old Danisha with her while she socialized with friends. Tina's mother stayed in an alcove removed from the reception and did not mingle with the other guests. I came upon them as her mother was sitting alone with Danisha. Despite her frailty, she was holding Danisha up in front of her face, gazing at her with a beatific smile on her skeletal face, basking in delight at her grandchild. Tina's mother died just four months later.

"I just thank God that she got to see Danisha. She got to hold her."

The Gift

I could not give you my life;
The anger was too strong between us.
I can not give you your life;
The virus will not let go.
But I can give you this life,
This new and perfect reflection of yourself.
Hold her; look at her
And know that you will live
Even after you have passed on.

(A poem I wrote after seeing Tina's mother holding Danisha)

Tina explicitly told me that she saw Danisha as a replacement for her mother. She remembered that she had gotten pregnant for the first time when her father died. Her second pregnancy, which she terminated under duress, occurred right after her aunt disclosed that her mother had AIDS. She became pregnant with Danisha just four months after that. In fact, the timing of all three of Tina's pregnancies suggests that they may be, at some level, a response to the loss or impending loss of her parents. Tina herself put this eloquently.

"I look at Danisha and, I think about that saying. They say that God will always give a life before He takes a life. He gave me Danisha in replace of my mother."

Amid the turmoil and loss Tina experienced, Danisha also provided a reason for her to be strong. The baby needed her, and this gave her purpose and a reason to set her own troubles aside. Tina said that Danisha kept her from attempting suicide again because she felt responsible for her.

"Only thing that I say to this day, and I thank God for it, is Danisha. I thank God. If I go, where is she gonna be at? And is she gonna be ok and everything."

As in many teen pregnancies, the baby was an achievement for Tina. She had produced something good and valuable, something that marked her successful transition to womanhood in the community. This was especially meaningful for Tina, as she had experienced a great deal of failure in school and had been in special education for much of her life. The role of mother gave Tina a status and importance that was difficult, if not impossible to achieve otherwise. Tina expressed the significance of being a mother as, "I'm the most important one in her life."

Sadly, Tina had little experience with successful mothering. The role of mother was tainted because of her poor relationship with her own mother, and Tina didn't want to reenact that relationship with Danisha. In spite of criticism from her sisters and others, she insisted that Danisha call her Tina instead of Mommy. She felt her daughter would become estranged from her if she assumed a mother's role but would feel closer if she were more like a big sister.

Tina's hopes for her relationship with her daughter did not take the baby's needs into account and quickly proved unrealistic. When her sisters planned to move to Georgia, Tina recounted the litany of her losses, but she consoled herself with the fact that she had her daughter. Then she poignantly voiced her disappointment that her baby could not give her the love and companionship she needed.

"She says her little words to me, like her baby talk, or whatever. But, she's not a person I could sit and conversate with. It really bothers me. That she don't know no better. She's just a baby."

There was a profound sadness in her expression of loneliness and longing for a companion. She had hoped her baby would fill this role, but she could not.

Despite the significance and hope that Danisha brought to Tina, she could not fill the void in her life.

"I'm So Confused, I Don't Know What to Do."

"At times I be wanting to pull my hair out. To just, go crazy."

Tina told me that after her mother's death she began to experience a number of problems. She said she had alienated a lot of people, who complained that she had a perpetually bad attitude. A rift developed between her and Ramon's sister Marisol because she was increasingly intolerant of Ramon's behavior and was withholding Danisha from him. Tina reported to me that she was more angry and impatient with people, although she did not act that way in our interviews. She also complained about becoming forgetful and misplacing things. She felt that her characteristic difficulty talking about her feelings was making it harder for her to cope with her mother's death.

"There's a lot that I still don't let out. And that's why I be feeling the way that I feel. I was always the type that don't tell nobody how I feel. I still am like that."

Tina also felt that her problems following her mother's death were affecting her parenting of Danisha.

"But like, if I hit Danisha or if I yell at her, I'll hug her real quick, because I'll be concerned. Cause, I'm missing my mother a lot, and I took everything out on her."

"Ain't Nothing Else to Do but Be Alright."

Perhaps one thing that made it hard for Tina to talk about her problems was her belief that some things were better left unsaid. Why complain when help was usually not forthcoming? In spite of Tina's neediness, she was careful not to demand too much from others in terms of attention or material aid, especially from people who were not intimates. She kept her expectations low and didn't complain when even these were not met. Besides, complaining ran the risk of alienating possible benefactors. In the end, some things just had to be endured, unless you could change them yourself.

After her mother's death Tina lost her supported apartment because she persisted in allowing Ramon to stay there, against the rules. She lived with her sisters in her mother's old apartment for awhile, but they fought, and her older sister told her to leave. Having also alienated Ramon's family, Tina found herself with nowhere to live, and she and Danisha entered a homeless shelter. While conditions were less than optimal, instead of bewailing her fate, Tina told me, "You can't ask for a lot." She accepted that she would have to live in the shelter for at least six months in order to qualify for permanent housing.

In spite of her many troubles: the loss of both her parents, her problems with boyfriends, the difficulties of parenting, and her ongoing searches for a home, Tina often maintained the appearance that everything was alright. Her outwardly optimistic response to problems was illustrated when she reassured her jailhouse beau that they would continue to communicate even if her phone was cut off. Her solution, while upbeat and sweet spirited, was somewhat unrealistic considering her reading disability.

"I said, 'But there's pen and paper.' And he said, 'You go girl!'"

But when she was confronted with the reality of their separation, she had a different reaction. "I felt like it was the end of the world. He stopped calling me."

"God Let It Happen."

Tina was not a very religious person, but she invoked God's name frequently, especially as a way to explain why things happened. She maintained that God was in charge and that some things happened through His intervention, rather than through her own agency. God for her was a benevolent presence who kept a balance between life and death and caused things to work out for the best.

Tina's most profound sense of God was in the meaning she ascribed to her pregnancies. Her belief that God gave her Danisha in exchange for her mother helped her to cope with her loss.

> They say that God will always give a life before He takes a life . . . And I
> believe that. Because, when my father passed, is when I got pregnant the first
> time. So, I thought He gave me a life for a life. And the same now, with my
> mother and Danisha.

Her perspective that her mother's death was a release from suffering helped her to accept that as well. "I had to understand, that when she go, God was only taking her, instead of having her in pain and suffering. So I understood it like that."

Tina had been very concerned that her mother might die in her apartment. She felt it was God who allowed her mother to die in the hospital, sparing her daughters the gruesome task of dealing with her body. Tina expressed thanks for this.

It was painful for Tina to visit her mother in the hospital. Her mother wasn't able to talk and, "they had lots of tubes in her. I didn't want to go see her." Tina knew that when the doctors disconnected the life support system her mother would probably die. She had left a message to that effect on my telephone at work the day before her mother died. Perhaps on some level Tina did not want to have to go through the pain of being present at her mother's deathbed. It's hard to tell, because Tina took no responsibility for not going to see her. She told me that she believed that God was responsible for keeping her away from her mother's deathbed.

"I always say God kept me from it. Cause I was supposed to go see my mother that day . . . And then, I didn't get nowhere! I stood there still. I didn't know what for. I knew nothing."

Because of God's intervention she could remain unaware of her feelings and not take responsibility for her choice.

Tina thanked God for indirectly safeguarding her own life by giving her the responsibility of caring for Danisha. She said that her concern over Danisha's well being was the major reason for her not to attempt suicide.

" I think about suicide from time to time. Only thing that I say to this day, and I thank God for it, is Danisha. I thank God. Because, if I go, where is she gonna be at? Is she gonna be ok and everything?"

God did not just intervene in matters of life and death. He also presided in matters of love. Despite Tina's negative experiences with lovers, she hoped that God would send her a good man to love. In the flush of her telephone romance with her jailhouse beau she told me, "After all I been through, I feel like God is just now finally sending me the right one."

For Tina, God provided a way to explain things, a way to accept her mother's illness and death, a reason for her actions that did not require her to be aware of her feelings or to take responsibility, and a sense of hope.

"I Always Say . . . "

Tina frequently used the word "always" to take a statement out of the realm of everyday fact and mythologize it. Such statements seemed to represent more the wish for something than the fact, and they cannot be judged by the standards of what actually happened. Even though Tina fought with her mother and seldom lived with her from the age of fifteen, she told me, "I always say, my mother was there for us," and, "We always stayed with my mother."

"Always" seemed to confer certainty to an explanation, as when Tina talked about her absence from her mother's deathbed, "I always say God kept me from it." The "always" in this statement seemed to provide an emphasis that rendered the statement indisputable, regardless of the circumstances surrounding the event.

Tina created self soothing narratives about her life and the people close to her. While the creation of personal narratives is a strategy by which we all attempt to make sense of our lives, it is noteworthy that in her narratives Tina tended to magnify positive, supportive behavior and downplay negative events.

A striking contradiction in her story is that between the words of support with which she characterized her mother, her father, Ramon, and even herself, in contrast to their actions of neglect and abandonment. She seemed to experience people as helping her when they actually didn't. Or perhaps she was trying to convince herself and her listeners that they did. It is as though she tried to create support and satisfying relationships with words, even though the evidence of what she reported actually happened suggested otherwise. It seemed to me that Tina did this, not so much to keep up appearances, although this was important to her, as to soothe herself and create satisfying relationships in place of discord and loss.

When Tina was pregnant with Danisha her mother said she would help her, and Tina moved back in with her. Within two months they were fighting again, and her mother told her she had to move out. Even though their reconciliation was shortlived, Tina emphasized the support she had felt from her mother and glossed over the discord between them.

"She took me in after everything I put her through. She took me back in. I stayed with her. But I moved out again. But I always stayed in touch with her."

When I asked Tina how she thought her mother contracted HIV, she replied by first denying her mother had been at risk for HIV and painting a portrait of a quiet, retiring person. "You would never think my mother would get AIDS. She was not a person that used to party." These factors may have been true, but they ignore the real risk factor faced by her mother, her longstanding intravenous drug use, which was confirmed by Tina's former teacher.

Tina tried to find the silver lining in even the worst situations. A year before she died, Tina's mother tried to commit suicide by jumping out of her apartment window. She landed in some bushes and was severely injured and hospitalized for several weeks. Tina at first expressed great remorse that she had been in school and hadn't been home to prevent it. A week later she wondered whether her mother had jumped out of the window head first or feet first. She reasoned that if it were feet first perhaps she hadn't really intended to kill herself.

Tina cherished the memory of her father, even though he did not appear to have provided much support to her. She preserved love and regard for him by not expecting too much from him.

> He walked, in and out of our life. He was the type of father that promised something, but if he didn't give it, we didn't always be like, but you promised. More or less he was there, but he gave us his love. That was good enough for us.

It is ironic that she felt closest to him when he wasn't really around when she was growing up. In a way his death prevented any estrangement because it enabled her to hold on to her cherished memories of him without him making demands on her or disappointing her further. His death permitted her to maintain the illusion of his care.

Similarly, Tina wanted Ramon to support their baby, but sometimes just the illusion of support seemed to suffice. If her baby's father couldn't be depended upon for support, she would prop him up, if necessary, just as she had propped up her unreliable father in her own mind.

"I tell him, I can always buy Danisha something, and it could be from you, and you can always give it to her."

Despite the fact that Ramon had abandoned them, she told me how she explained his absence to Danisha. "I always say, 'Daddy be home soon. He's out to the store.'"

Tina savored the illusion of support from her jailhouse beau, "He told me I would never have to worry about needing nothing. He's always gonna give it to me. Even now, if I need something, all I got to do is just tell him. He'll have somebody give it to me." This strained credulity, but Tina, usually very savvy and streetwise, chose to accept it.

The illusion of support was maintained though other strategies such as declining offers of help. Tina responded to her jailhouse beau's offer of support with, "That's ok. My check is enough." Her undemanding self-sufficiency allowed him to posture about taking care of her without actually having to do anything, and it sustained the myth of his supportiveness. She expressed no irony or disappointment that he did not offer to help her pay for her phone bill, even though the disconnection of her phone cut off their only means of communication.

Tina created narratives to explain her own actions as well. She was absent from her mother's deathbed, but her story about her mother's death helped her to feel both that she was present in a very intimate way and that she had been spared the anguish of that moment. "I always say God kept me from it." Tina told me the story of her mother's death with a sense of shared participation in the experience, as though she had been there. Although she was at home when her mother died, she experienced it in an immediate and intimate way through her "premonition" of her mother's passing.

Tina's narratives of support propped up significant others, like her mother, her father, Ramon, her jailhouse beau, and even herself. She maintained the illusion of support by not asking for much, keeping her distance, withdrawing when no help was forthcoming, and magnifying the little help her intimates did give with her stories. Her words created stories that sustained the illusion of satisfying relationships and support that were strikingly absent in her life.

"A Man Is Gonna Go, but I'm Looking for the Right One."

Tina appeared to derive a great deal of pleasure in talking about her relationships with her boyfriends. Love seemed to be for her an intoxicant that made her forget about her other problems. Despite repeated disappointments she still found excitement and respite in love. She maintained her hope for love despite the fact that she believed that, "A man is gonna go." This aphorism had been told her by her mother, and it accurately reflected her experiences with her father and all her boyfriends. Yet she also told me about her jailhouse beau, "After all I been through, I feel like God is just now finally sending me the right one," implying the hope that certain relationships, arranged by God, were meant to last.

Tina had come upon a novel arrangement which enabled her to savor the romantic aspect of love without many of the pitfalls of relationships. She became engaged in two consecutive telephone romances with men she had not previously met in person. These liaisons were extremely exciting for her. They seemed to prolong the courtship phase of the relationship and give Tina a chance to talk and be listened to. Her inaccessibility to her lover, while at the same time being able to talk intimately, enabled her to feel desired without having to cope with actual physical demands or the emotional vicissitudes of everyday life.

CHAPTER V

Common Themes

The themes for each of the participants were abstracted from their stories, which in turn were crafted from their interviews. Their themes seem for the most part idiosyncratic and reflect the individual participants' personal philosophies and ways of coping with life. Maria was fierce and full of rage. Tina attempted to preserve an illusion of caring and support. Joe operated on the "down low" to avoid impediments to his pursuit of self gratification.

On another level, their themes also reflect the participants' responses to the devastating crisis of AIDS in their family and the more insidious but even more damaging effects of their mothers' drug addiction. While we cannot generalize from the experience of these three individuals, it is useful to examine commonalities and differences in their stories in order to gain some insight into the experience of having a mother who suffered from AIDS.

"WE'RE OUT HERE BY OURSELVES"

The most apparent commonality among the young people who shared their stories with me was their lack of a stable home. All three had moved repeatedly during their mothers' illness and in prior years as well. Maria had lived with her parents, with her grandmother and with several drug dealers before coming to the Center. Joe had lived with several caretakers while his mother was incarcerated, and after her release he lived first with her and then at the Center. Tina lived with her mother only sporadically from the time she was fifteen and stayed with whatever friends would have her.

During the course of our interviews all three participants each moved again at least once. Joe lived with his mother in a hotel; they then moved to an apartment. He told me he was planning to move back to the Center at our last interview. Maria lived alternately with her stepfather and with her boyfriend's family. During the ten months she participated in the study, Tina lived with her older sister, her friend Marisol, in a homeless shelter, and in her own apartment. After our last formal interview she left the East Coast for California.

The lack of a stable home was not a recent phenomenon for these young people, rather it was a longstanding situation. It appeared to stem from problems related to their mothers' drug abuse, as well as their inability to get along with them. All three teenagers experienced extreme conflict with their mothers, to the point where they all chose to leave home. Maria was the most direct in verbalizing this, "I wanted to live with her, but I couldn't. Cause we always fight. We never got along." Sarah told me that Maria, "was on the streets when she was 13, living with drug dealers." Tina was the most circumspect about fighting with her mother and took the blame herself, "Whatever she said, I always did the opposite, or I always gave her backtalk about it." Unlike Maria and Joe, she never had a permanent alternative to her mother's house, and she repeatedly returned home, only to leave again after a few weeks or months. Joe, the only participant whose mother was living at the time of our interviews, talked at length about his on-going battles with his mother and how difficult it was to live with her.

The Center was a refuge for Maria and Joe from their intolerable home situations. They were attracted there by the presence of other teenagers from similar backgrounds. However, it was unlicensed and seemed to me to be dirty and disorganized. Although people inside the building were supposed to be drug free, the environment immediately outside the doors was not.

The lack of a stable home for these young people was further compounded by several other factors. Firstly, in both Tina's and Maria's families, other family members had contracted AIDS. Tina's aunt died of AIDS during the time of our interviews. Maria's father had died of the disease several years prior to her mother's death. In both families the common risk factor was intravenous drug use. This loss of close adult family members meant that there were fewer housing options available for the teens during their mothers' illness or after she had passed away.

A second factor which complicated the issue of a stable home was the resistance on the part of all three teens to accepting limits. All three lost housing in social service organizations set up to help young people because they chose not to follow the rules. Joe's pursuit of self gratification "on the down low" without regard for the Center's rules resulted in his being asked to leave. Maria left the Center by choice because she "didn't want to hear it" from Sarah about her pregnancy. Tina lost her supported apartment because she repeatedly broke the rules by allowing her boyfriend to live with her.

Their lack of a stable home base and their resistance to accepting limits combined to create a quality of inaccessibility in these young people. On a physical level it was often very difficult to reach them because of their frequent moves and their lack of contact with their families. On an emotional level they were sometimes inaccessible to people who tried to help them because of their tendency to reject limits and to leave a place that offered shelter and care rather than try to work out problems.

"MY MOTHER HAD A PROBLEM"

All three of the participants' mothers had abused heroin and presumably contracted the virus by sharing needles, a common practice among intravenous drug users (Fernando, 1993 and McKeganey & Barnard, 1992). The sharing of intravenous needles for illegal drug use is only one route of transmission for HIV, and this common factor among the mothers of all three participants in this study in no way suggests that all women with AIDS who have adolescent children have abused drugs. It does coincide with the fact that, during the current phase of the AIDS epidemic, intravenous drug abuse is the most common risk category for the transmission of HIV to women in the city in which these young people lived. The New York City Department of Health reported that 56% of women with AIDS in the city had contracted HIV by intravenous drug use. The next highest transmission category for women in the city is sex with men who are infected with HIV, comprising 30% of women with AIDS (NYCDOH,1997).

Joe and Maria came from the Lower East Side and Tina from the South Bronx; both neighborhoods are notorious for their poverty, drug use and high rates of HIV infection. The rates for diagnosed cases of AIDS among adults on the Lower East Side is 2.5% and in the South Bronx it is 2.6%. Both these rates are well above the city's already high average of 1.5% of the adult population, as of April, 1997 (Ibid., p. 14).

In all three families there appeared to be a great deal of secrecy surrounding the mother's drug use, whether it derived from the mothers' efforts to conceal their behavior or the participants' reluctance to discuss it. Maria, the most outspoken about her mother's problems, stated that she hated her mother because she abused drugs. However, although her parents both used and sold drugs in the home, Maria told me that "I really never seen the drug exchange. Or drug use." Similarly, Joe admitted that, "My mother always did drugs," but when asked how his mother contracted HIV told me, "I think she got it because she was shooting up. I don't really know. I wasn't with the details." Sarah, the director of the Center where Joe lived told me that during the time of our interviews Joe's mother was abusing drugs again. This was a likely source of their conflict at that time, but Joe did not tell me about his mother's drug use. Tina was the most reluctant to talk about her mother's drug use. She told me, "I don't know if she shot drugs. That part she never told me." But when she ruled out any other risk factor for contracting HIV she concluded, "The only thing I can think of is drugs."

People who are addicted to heroin need to invest a great deal of time as well as emotional and financial resources to procure and use drugs, and while they are under the influence of the drugs their judgment is impaired. These factors are bound to have a significant and pervasively negative effect on their parenting and their relationship with their children. Maria felt that her mother's drug use caused her to physically abuse her. Joe's mother appears to have been neglectful, leaving him with unfamiliar, untrustworthy people when she went with her boyfriend to Puerto Rico. Tina rarely acknowledged her mother's drug use, but it seems likely to have played a major role in their conflict. For all three participants, the loss of their mother due to her illness or death from AIDS was nothing new. Because of the mothers' substance abuse and, in Joe's case resulting legal problems, their unavailability to their children seems to have been severe and longstanding. AIDS was only the final loss.

"ME AND MY MOTHER DIDN'T GET ALONG"

All three teenagers experienced extreme conflict with their mothers. It appears that even when the mothers stopped abusing drugs, the conflict endured. This discord does not seem to be only their children's continuing anger at their mother's past behavior, but rather on-going, reciprocal problems. For example, when Maria became pregnant for the first time, her mother was no longer using drugs, but her response seemed inordinately harsh. "How could you do this! You need to be locked up, to do this to me. I just can't believe you'd do something like this!" Apparently the rage between Maria and her mother existed on both sides of the relationship.

Early in our counseling relationship Tina told me how her mother threw her out of the house and put her clothes out on the fire escape. However, after she knew for sure that her mother had AIDS Tina downplayed their conflicts and tended to emphasize any supportive behavior on her mother's part. Even though they seemed to have stopped fighting, Tina still kept her distance from her mother, both emotionally and physically.

Joe talked at great length about fighting with his mother, and how difficult it was for him to live with her. However, he focused the cause of their discord on her intrusions into his room and did not mention her continued drug use.

Intense and unresolved conflict of the type described by all three participants might tend to be obscured by the emergency of their mothers' deteriorating health. After her death their sense of loss and grief would probably make it difficult to cope with negative feelings towards their mother. This could account for the ambivalence expressed by all three participants. These unresolved feelings would tend to complicate mourning.

"SOMETHING TO LIVE FOR"

In the face of the instability, conflict and lack of nurturing they had experienced, all three participants sought ways to sustain themselves and bring meaning and pleasure to their lives. Joe and Tina hoped for a better future, where they would find justice and love. Even Maria, the most deeply pessimistic of the three young people, had hope for better things, despite what she saw as the inherent unfairness of life. All three linked their hope for the future to their newborn babies. In the here and now they sought excitement and affirmation through romantic and/or sexual relationships.

All three participants had babies who were born within a year of their mother's deaths. Maria was comforted by the fact that her baby was due to be born on the anniversary of her mother's death. Tina's and Joe's babies were born a few months before their mothers' deaths, and both expressed gratitude that their mothers had lived to be able to see the baby.

On one level childbearing can be seen as a deeply human response to the loss of a parent. Giving birth to a child around the time of a parent's death may bring a sense of continuity. It can be an affirmation of the fact that life, and the family, will go on. Having a baby creates a new family in the face of the loss of the family of origin. Maria expressed it eloquently, "The baby, that's your mother being with you, or your father. Cause that's family."

The participants all spoke to the many meanings their babies had for them. For Joe and Tina the baby was a gift to their dying mother, a reassurance that she was "leaving something", that part of her would live on. Tina and Maria felt alone, and they hoped their babies would provide them with love and companionship. For all three the baby was an achievement and a possession, something that was uniquely theirs.

All three teens told me that their babies provided them with something to live for and gave meaning to their lives. They echoed each other's opinion that having a baby would help them to be more mature and responsible and would give them the impetus to change some of their self-defeating behaviors. Having a baby signified a passage to adulthood, and both Joe and Tina enjoyed the respect and attention the role of parent brought. However, both had great difficulty carrying out the attendant responsibilities.

These multiple meanings attached to having babies are not unique to these young people. Rather they are conventional ways many people invest the "blessed event" with meaning. The sad difference in this case is that these young people were unprepared to cope, both emotionally and practically, with the reality of a baby's needs. Moreover, they did not have the family support to help with this potentially overwhelming task. Although Joe was initially thrilled to be a father, by the time his daughter was two months old he confided that he sometimes felt like strangling her. He deeply resented the baby's mother for leaving the child with him on weekends. Joe said he could not cope with her, and her crying agitated his increasingly incapacitated mother. Tina told me how she sometimes hit her daughter because she felt stressed. She also frequently left the baby with other people for days at a time. Maria's baby was not yet born when we last spoke, but I brought up the question of child abuse with her because of her history of abuse and the fact that aggression was her characteristic response to stress. She acknowledged that adults who have been abused as children are more likely to abuse their own children, but she felt that she would be able to control herself. I do not know what happened after her baby was born.

The tragedy of these teenagers having babies is that they were grossly unprepared to be parents. None of them had had adequate parenting themselves, and they were already experiencing great difficulty coping with the stress and loss in their lives. Whatever solace and feelings of love and competence their babies brought them, they also added significantly more stress to their lives, as well as the potential for more failure and loss.

While babies signified hope for the future, romantic and sexual relationships were a primary way these young people sought happiness in the present. Again, this is an appropriate path to self fulfillment, especially for adolescents. However, it seemed to me that for these teens normal adolescent sexual attraction was accentuated to the point where it was almost an opiate, a preoccupation that helped to obscure other concerns. All three participants spoke at length and with great relish about their love lives. Joe considered himself a ladies' man and prided himself on his many sexual liaisons. Maria was embroiled in a triangular relationship complicated by the fact that no one knew for certain who was the father of her unborn child. She appeared to take pleasure in the intricacies of her predicament and the power she had to decide what roles she would allow her lovers to play. Tina savored the emotional aspect of her love relationships. She maintained her faith in true love, even though she had only experienced unsuccessful and sometimes abusive relationships. She discovered through long distance telephone relationships a means to accentuate and sustain the heady initial glow of love without subjecting it to the vicissitudes of everyday life. However, when she finally met her telephone lovers and interacted with them in person, the relationships soured rather quickly.

All three young people were admittedly sexually active with more than one partner. When I asked them about condom use, all three initially gave the impression they were using them. However they later admitted that frequently they were not. Joe was anxious about his indiscretions; Maria felt she probably should use condoms, but admitted she didn't. Tina sometimes used condoms at the beginning of a relationship but soon discontinued use, especially if there was any pressure from her lover.

Witnessing the ravages of AIDS first hand appeared to increase Joe's dread of contracting the disease himself. However, his fear of the disease did not promote consistently safe behavior, and he admitted to me "at least five" instances of unsafe sex with girls other than his steady girlfriend, with whom he never used a condom, despite her repeated infidelities.

Maria framed the necessity for condoms as an issue of trust. Rather than basing her decision on factual information and an assessment of risk factors, her willingness to engage in unprotected sex was based on her emotional attachment to her partner. If she loved the man she was with and felt she knew him, she did not use condoms, regardless of what she knew of his sexual history or his other current partners. Tina had similar attitudes. The fact that their mothers had died of AIDS did not appear to influence their decisions whether or not to use safer sex practices.

The one exception to this was when Tina allowed Ramon to sleep in her apartment after she discovered he was living with a new girlfriend. She refused to have sex with him and made him sleep out in the living room, saying to him that since his current girlfriend was a drug abuser, there was no telling what diseases he might have. I was heartened by her decision, but I suspect it had more to do with punishing him for living with the other woman than self preservation.

All three teens had very little in their lives which gave them cause for optimism. It is sadly ironic that the ways in which they sought happiness and hope for their future, through romantic or sexual relationships and childbearing, served to exacerbate their problems and put them at risk for contracting HIV themselves.

EPILOGUE: WHERE ARE THEY NOW?

I never saw Maria after her second interview. Joe and I met for two interviews. After that I saw him briefly when I was at the Center for Maria's second interview. I never saw him after that. I tried to follow up with both of them, at least for participant checks, so I could get their opinions of the sense I had made of their stories. However, I was unable to locate either one of them.

I tried to reach Maria through her stepfather, but he told me she no longer stayed there, and he did not know where to reach her. He told me she had had a baby boy, instead of the girl she told me she would have preferred. That was all I knew about her, until about a year later, when a staff member at her former school told me some of the other students had seen Maria in the red light district. She was performing in a peep show. No one knew where Maria was living or whether she was still together with her child.

Joe's mother died a few months after our last interview. He stopped living at the Center, and there was no other number at which to contact him. According to his former Assistant Principal, Joe began using drugs again and dropped out of school.

Tina maintained contact with me after her move to the West Coast. She had relationship problems with the man she'd gone to California to live with, including infidelity on both parts and physical abuse. They both came back to New York and stayed at various locations. I was looking forward to meeting with her around Christmas, but she failed to keep our appointment, and I had no number to reach her. She called me a few weeks later and told me she had gone to a psychiatric emergency room because of suicidal thoughts. Several weeks later she called me from a shelter for battered women and told me she was doing well. She said that the shelter would lead to an apartment, but she couldn't give me a number to reach her because of the shelter's rules. I got the feeling that she was "working the system" to get an apartment. I was pleased that she had accessed resources. She had always been good at that; her problem has been holding on to what she has. She told me she was considering legally signing over Danisha to a friend to raise until she could "get my head together." She said her caseworker felt it would be best for Danisha if she did so. My last contact with Tina to date was a telephone message in which she sounded a little distressed but, typically, told me she "can't complain" about how things are going for her. She did not leave a number where I could reach her.

CHAPTER VI

Discussion and Implications

The results of this study are not meant to be generalized and to speak for all, or even most adolescents and young adults whose mothers have AIDS or have died of the disease. This study is an attempt to gain a deeper understanding of the experiences and perspectives of a few young people in this situation. Rather than attempting to generalize to others, I hope to be able to illuminate their experience and their perceptions of their lives. This in turn may provide insight into the problems of some other AIDS affected youth and lead to an understanding of how best to assist them. In qualitative research the issue of whether findings can be applied in other settings is called transferability (Lincoln & Guba, 1985). Qualitative researchers can address this issue by providing information that may be judged by others in similar situations to be useful. My attempt here is to present such information.

In many ways, the stories of the participants of this study mirrored the findings of the few other studies of AIDS affected youth discussed in the Review of Literature section. Joe, Maria and Tina described from their perspectives many of the characteristics of AIDS affected youth cited in the literature, such as frequent changes in residence, behavior problems, and risky sexual behavior with multiple partners. Similarly, the problems with disclosure in their families reflected those discussed in the literature, which reported the difficulties many families have with revealing the parent's diagnosis.

UNSTABLE LIVING ARRANGEMENTS

All three had experienced unstable and frequently changing living arrangements and still struggled with the issue of finding a place to live. None of the three felt that living at home with their mother, while she was alive, was a viable option. Their intense, on-going conflicts with their mothers precluded that. Joe, who was living with his mother at the time of our interviews, described how his arguments with her incensed him to the point where he felt compelled to move out, even though he knew she would soon die.

When their mothers died both Tina and Maria returned to their mother's former apartment to live. Tina stayed only briefly because her older sister, who had taken over the lease and was caring for their younger sister, asked her to leave. The problem centered around Tina's refusal to follow basic household rules. She would stay away for days at a time and not let her sisters know where she was. Maria's mother's apartment had been taken over by her step-father, and Maria returned there when she left the Center. Like Tina, Maria did not get along with the surviving family members inhabiting the apartment. She lived with them only sporadically and stayed at her boyfriend's house for extended periods. She was looking forward to having her own apartment once her baby was born.

The participants did not fare well with alternative housing arrangements either. Conflict and defiance of rules were not limited to interactions with their mothers or family members. All three participants left or were asked to leave housing run by formal or informal social service organizations because of rule infractions. In all three cases the problem could have been rectified by their compliance with the rules or even by simply discussing the infraction. However, all three young people chose to leave. Maria voiced the feelings of the three with her comment, "I don't want to hear nothing!" She did not want other people telling her what to do. Joe was quieter but resisted the rules nonetheless, proclaiming, "I just want to chill," or relax. He felt living was difficult enough for him, and he saw no reason to stress himself to comply with rules. Tina did not talk about her feelings about breaking rules, but when the rules at her supported apartment conflicted with her desire to let her boyfriend stay with her, she simply persisted letting him stay until she was asked to leave. She did not voice any feelings of loss or regret, even though her boyfriend abandoned her as soon as she had no apartment to offer.

Whether they characteristically challenged or disregarded the rules, the resultant clash and loss of a place to stay was similar for all three participants, and all three repeatedly found themselves without a place to live. Their perspectives on this experience make it apparent that their homelessness problem could not be solved only by providing foster homes, group homes or other housing arrangements. The issues of resistance to limits and the balance between responsibility and autonomy must be addressed in order to make any living arrangement work.

The literature (Dane & Miller, 1992; Draimin et al., 1992; Hudis, 1995; Levine & Stein,1994; and Zayas & Romano, 1994) reports that while younger children in an AIDS affected family may be taken in by relatives or foster families, custody poses particular problems for adolescents. Not only are they less desirable than children, but their behavior problems, like the propensity to challenge or disregard limits that the three participants of this study spoke of, make them difficult to live with. A potential guardian may agree to take the children in a family but reject the adolescent(s). Unable to find a home, but not yet able to be self supporting, teen survivors of AIDS are often left with no place to go. Young women who become pregnant and start a family of their own can receive support, including an apartment through Public Assistance. Young men do not have similar options.

Emotional Inaccessibility

The sheer number of times that the participants and the other AIDS affected adolescents I tried to recruit for the study moved was daunting and had ramifications in many areas of their lives. For one thing, their recurrent moves frequently rendered them inaccessible. I found this to be a significant problem, and I often had difficulty in reaching them. Even more problematic is my impression that their physical inaccessibility reflected an emotional inaccessibility. All three participants at times dealt with problems by withdrawing rather than trying to work them out. Maria chose to leave the safe haven of the Center rather than reveal and discuss her pregnancy with Sarah. Joe and Tina seemed to me to withhold information and feelings during our interviews. This was evident with Joe whenever he declined to speak with me about topics which were uncomfortable for him, as described in his theme, "I don't like to tell about it." When he did discuss emotionally laden topics he was often very vague and did not elaborate when I asked for more information.

Perhaps it is understandable that Joe did not share more with me. I only met him during our interviews and was otherwise an unknown to him. However, Tina also withheld important pieces of information and sometimes chose not to delve into difficult topics with me, even when I was her counselor. Although I felt we had a good counseling relationship, and Tina shared many intimate details of her life with me, she did not tell me that her mother had AIDS for approximately six months after she learned for certain of her mother's condition.

The participants' reluctance to talk about some major issues made it frustrating for me as a researcher and, in my counseling relationship with Tina, as a helping professional. As a researcher I wanted to know more so I could understand the participants' experiences and effectively describe and analyze them. As a counselor I realized that my feelings of efficacy and my perceptions of the bond I had made with my counselees were both threatened when information was withheld. When I was Tina's counselor I had always made a point of not taking her negative behavior personally. I set limits with her, which enabled me not to personalize her acting out, as many of her teachers did. When a teacher felt disappointed in her it usually resulted in an acrimonious power struggle similar to those Tina described in her relationship with her mother. I was successful in avoiding these. However after our counseling relationship was over I learned that a teacher who had known Tina some years before knew of her mother's drug addiction. I felt hurt. This was not just the acting out behavior I had learned to deal with, but something that I felt reflected on our counseling relationship. After all we had gone through together, why did she choose not to openly discuss it with me? Why did a teacher know when I, her counselor, did not?

I dealt with those feelings and realized that it was probably easier for Tina to share information about her mother's drug use before there was any indication of her illness. However, a lesson that I have drawn from my participants and my experiences with Tina is that it is important for helping professionals working with AIDS affected youth to be aware of the possibility that, despite our best intentions and practices, some young people may be resistant to talking about topics that relate to their mothers' illness or addiction. We have to acknowledge this and understand our own countertransference reactions to it. It is essential that we do not take personally their resistance to talking about distressing issues. We need to see our job as helping the teens to meet their needs, rather than wanting them to meet our expectations so we can feel like good counselors. My experience with Tina has also shown me that addressing the very urgent practical needs of AIDS affected young people, such as housing, is a priority, and that this can lead to increased trust and sharing of "secrets".

Perhaps an advantage of both the physical and emotional inaccessibility that I experienced with the participants is that these may have given the young people the feeling of having more control over their lives, especially in their interpersonal interactions. Their inaccessibility certainly created difficulties for people trying to reach them, but the young people could unilaterally initiate contact or reply to messages. This one-sidedness may have provided a sort of emotional insulation. Unfortunately, a big disadvantage to their inaccessibility is that it also served to isolate them, leaving them emotionally and physically alone at the very time they most needed support.

The participants' intermittent homelessness reflected not only a lack of a stable place to stay, but also a lack of consistent nurturing and emotional support. Maria and Joe were clear about the deprivations of their early years and how their needs were not met. Maria made a virtue out of her necessity to stand alone and support herself, even though she was not yet able to do this in a safe and constructive way. Tina tried to paint a happier picture, but it appears that all three of them lacked sufficient support as children. Perhaps they now rejected some assistance and the limits it implied because, having been bereft of these supports in their most vulnerable years, they hadn't derived any benefits from them and now experienced them as confining and a threat to their independence.

Perhaps if their most urgent needs were met in a reliable fashion they might learn that sometimes it can be safe to trust. I think that AIDS affected young people need to be provided with concrete, meaningful support that addresses their self-identified needs and gives leeway for their developmentally appropriate striving for independence. In this way perhaps they can learn to accept the responsibility and attendant constraints on their behavior which are necessary for their safety and for getting along with other people.

BEHAVIOR AND LEARNING PROBLEMS

The literature (Dane & Miller; Draimin et al.; Hudis; Levine & Stein; Rotheram-Borus, 1995; and Zayas & Romano) discussed behavior problems exhibited by AIDS affected adolescents. These include problems at school, run-ins with the law, truancy and staying out all night or for days at a time. Maria, Joe, and Tina all described to me similar problems from their own perspectives. Maria talked at length about her anger and her propensity to externalize her pain by fighting and destroying property. Although she experienced her aggression as problematic, as when she felt driven to go out and hurt someone, she also experienced a sense of power in her ferocity. When she was a small child she had suffered her mother's rages, but as a young woman she was determined not to take abuse from anyone anymore. She seemed to have solved her problem by identifying with the aggressor and becoming abusive herself. Maria's extreme aggression reflected, and seems to have originated in her mother's abusive treatment of her. It may have served to counteract feelings of helplessness in the face of both her past abuse and her parents' illness and deaths. She told me she identified with her mother in her anger and belligerence. In addition to making her feel less vulnerable to the aggression of others, her own violent behavior may have served to foster an intimate connection between her and her deceased mother.

Maria's anger seemed to energize her. She seldom expressed sorrow, even when talking about very sad events in her life, but when she discussed anger she grew vivid and fierce. She described her destructive rampage in school and at her grandmother's house when she learned of her father's death. Instead of expressing sorrow she destroyed her surroundings. This acting out appears to have served both to express and to shield her from the intense pain of losing her father. I had the feeling that if Maria gave into sad feelings she might become very depressed. She alluded to this with her discussion of her marijuana smoking. Although she feared she might be hurting her unborn baby by using drugs, she told me that she felt she "had to". It was a kind of self medication, both to banish sad thoughts and to even out her rages, so she did not get into trouble.

When I first met Tina she told me about her fights with her mother and with peers. She also described a feeling of identification with her mother through her stubbornness and oppositionalism. However, her belligerent behavior appeared to decrease around the time her aunt told her that her mother had AIDS. She began to be more internalizing in her expression of her feelings. Instead of lashing out she tended to turn inward. She attempted suicide on at least one occasion. After her mother's death she described to me her problems with concentration and memory, suggesting depression. In addition, Tina had longstanding trouble with schoolwork, which she found arduous and unpleasant. Her problems were perhaps exacerbated by what had been diagnosed as a learning disability. Sometimes her feelings of alienation because of her mother's AIDS and her preoccupation with her predicament and distressing interpersonal issues within the family kept her from attending in class. Tina's living situation further compromised her school performance. Her frequent changes of residence contributed to her erratic attendance.

Joe also had learning problems and had a history of truancy when he lived with his mother. Like Maria, his behavior tended to be externalized, but he was more low-keyed than she was. His transgressions were, as he stated, on the down low, clandestine rather than in your face. He sold and used drugs when he lived with his mother. While he lived in the Center he participated in a burglary, and he frequently broke the Center rules by sneaking girls into his room, where he engaged in unprotected sex. Joe indicated to me that his sexual exploits gave him feelings of both pleasure and self worth.

UNSAFE SEXUAL BEHAVIOR

All three participants told me that they had had sexual relations with various partners without protection. Unprotected sex, at times with multiple partners is described in the literature (Demb, 1989; Draimin et al.; Hudis; and Rotheram-Borus, 1995) as common among AIDS affected adolescents. It is a very serious issue because it can expose them to STDs and HIV and can cause unintended pregnancy. It is important to understand the factors that support high risk sexual behavior. Judging from the perceptions that the participants shared with me, these factors are complex and seem to include anxiety, homelessness, a desire for pleasure and respite from their problems, and a wish for, or at least the acceptance of childbearing at this time in their lives. Some other contributing factors might include feelings of insufficient personal effectiveness to prevent exposure to HIV and STDs and a lack of limits elsewhere in their lives.

Programs to promote safer sexual behavior must address three different areas: increase in knowledge, change in attitudes and change in behavior (Kirby, 1984). It was clear from what the young people told me that a lack of knowledge was not the problem in their unsafe choices. Yet there was a definite failure to integrate what they knew on an intellectual level about safer sex and what they had experienced of the devastation of AIDS in their families into any consistent modification of their own sexual behavior.

One of the attitudinal factors underlying safer sex behavior is the perception that one is at risk for contracting an STD or HIV. Concern about personal vulnerability to HIV did not seem to be lacking among the participants. Joe, in particular, gave many paralinguistic signs of anxiety, such as a strangulated voice quality, when discussing his failures to follow safer sex practices. He was clearly worried, but the fact that he had not contracted a sexually transmitted disease (that he knew of) temporarily assuaged him. Ironically, the anxiety engendered by the participants' intimate acquaintance with the ravages of AIDS might have impaired their adaptive functioning and actually prevented them from taking steps to protect themselves. This can occur when a threat seems so overwhelming that it evokes maladaptive defenses such as denial (Novaco, 1979), which could lead to increased risk behaviors. All three young people at times evinced some denial of the riskiness of their sexual behavior.

Apprehension of risk is only one factor in mobilizing an individual to engage in risk reduction behaviors. Another is a sense of personal efficacy (Bandura, 1986, 1989; Brooks-Gunn, Boyer & Hein, 1988; Rotheram-Borus & Koopman, 1991). In order to take steps to prevent exposure, individuals must believe that, through their own actions, they can control whether or not they are exposed to the virus. Given their lack of success in other areas of their lives, the AIDS affected youth in the study may not have believed they could effectively protect themselves. They may have felt fatalistic about their chance of contracting a disease which had already infected at least one member of their immediate family.

Homelessness adds another dimension to the problem of risky sexual behavior. An important issue for both the AIDS affected youth in this study and in the literature is their intermittent but on-going search for a place to live. This can increase sexual risk, as some teens may engage in "survival sex" (Rotheram-Borus & Koopman, 1992), bartering sex for a place to stay. Before coming to the Center, Maria had lived with a series of drug dealers and was dependent on them for a place to stay because she did not want to go back home to her mother. Before she moved in with Marisol's family Tina had also lived sporadically with various young men whenever she left home.

The scarcity or rejection of limits elsewhere in the lives of this study's participants may also have been a factor in their failure to practice safer sex. Safer sex practices demand planning, discipline, and a modicum of self denial. Not only did the participants lack the opportunity to practice these qualities in other situations, but they often actively resisted limits. This might tend to make it more difficult to impose limits in such an intense and emotionally laden area as sexual behavior.

Another aspect of this problem is that, for the three young people in the study, romantic and sexual liaisons seemed to be a refuge from the rest of their problem-filled lives. It was one of the few arenas in which they seemed to feel pleasure and self worth. It also seemed to me to be such an intense preoccupation for the three as to screen out, if only briefly, other, more troublesome aspects of their lives. This may have given them respite from their problems, but it may have also contributed to their failure to integrate information about safer sex. Planning and performing safer sex practices could have introduced thoughts of AIDS into their love lives and might be experienced as unwelcome reminders of the crisis in their families which they were seeking to avoid.

AIDS can be a very anxiety provoking topic for AIDS affected youth, especially in public discussions. Tina described feelings of alienation and distress in Sex Education class when AIDS was being discussed. Instead of attending to the lesson, she described being consumed with anger at the perceived ignorance of her classmates, whom she felt did not understand that AIDS is not passed by casual contact. She knew this lesson well and did not fear becoming infected by her mother. However, she did fear being ostracized by classmates if they found out her mother had AIDS, because she felt they would consider her infectious as well. Attention needs to be paid to the issues of AIDS affected youth in Sex Education classes. Their privacy must be respected, and they should not fear being identified, but their pain and isolation need to be acknowledged and addressed. This could relieve them from solitary and distancing preoccupation with their predicament and enable them to attend to valuable information on prevention, which applies to them as well as to all other sexually active or potentially sexually active people.

Childbearing

Another aspect of the sexual risk taking of the young people in the study is the issue of pregnancy. Childbearing was a striking theme among the study participants, as well as among many of the adolescents affected by AIDS in my counseling practice. These were not really "unwanted" pregnancies, even though the young parents were generally not prepared to cope with their infants. The manifold significance of the participants' babies, as detailed in the analysis section of this paper, demonstrates their importance to the young people. Having babies seemed to offer the promise of filling the holes in their lives left by their many losses. Even if the babies were not consciously sought, once conceived they were accepted and valued for the many benefits they brought the young parent. The babies were gifts and replacements for the youths' ailing or deceased mothers, achievements, possessions, family, and reasons to have hope for the future. Given these perceptions of childbearing, birth control was not an issue that had much resonance for the young people. In fact, the desire to have a baby, whether consciously considered or not, would seem to militate against using birth control and thus to increase risky sexual behavior.

Childbearing by AIDS affected youth creates other problems and needs. Chief among these is the need for support and education in parenting. The young people in this study had all experienced serious conflict with their parents and deprivation in their upbringing. None of them had dependable people close to them on whom they could rely for support and advice in child care. Joe's commitment to his daughter waned abruptly when he became frustrated by his inability to care for her. Tina was also frustrated by her daughter, and Maria, because of her aggressiveness and history of abuse was at risk for abusing her child. The promise of fulfillment the babies offered paled beside the burden of their needs, which the young people were especially ill equipped to meet. These circumstances, compounded by the young people's inaccessibility and difficulty with limits, set the stage for continuing conflict and loss in their lives.

MULTIPLE LOSSES

The literature talks of the multiple losses suffered by most AIDS affected youth (Draimin et al, 1992; Levine & Stein, 1994), and Maria, Tina and Joe are no exceptions. Both Maria and Tina had other close family members who died of AIDS, and Tina's father had met a violent death when she was fifteen years old. Both Maria and Tina told me they "knew" when their fathers and mothers died even before they had been told. These premonitions seemed to me to be expressions of intimate connection with their deceased parents and the events of their deaths. Perhaps they also reflected a confirmation of the two young women's on-going expectations of loss.

Before he knew of his mother's illness, Joe lost her for several years while she was incarcerated. Right after she went to jail Joe's aunt threw him out of her house and refused to be involved with him. Even though he was in desperate need of a place to live he and his mother were abandoned by the extended family. It is unclear what happened to his father, because Joe never mentioned him.

All three mothers had been addicted to heroin, and this took a toll on their relationship with their children. For all three study participants, the deprivation of their mother had been longstanding, because of her addiction and their troubled relationship with her. AIDS was only the final, irrevocable loss.

DISCLOSURE

Disclosure of the mother's AIDS diagnosis had been a problem in the households of all three study participants. Maria's mother refused to disclose her diagnosis right up to her death. Her death certificate stated that she died of "natural causes", even though she was only thirty-seven years old. Her denial of her condition infuriated Maria and contributed significantly to their failure to reconcile after the mother overcame her heroin addiction.

In spite of the fact that Maria knew her mother had AIDS, her mother's failure to discuss her illness with her and the attribution of her death to natural causes on her death certificate appear to have created some confusion in Maria's mind as to the actual cause of her death. Maria told me that her mother's death was due to the stress of her efforts at rehabilitation and that she hadn't been sick when she died. This angered Maria and caused despair over what she saw as the futility of rehabilitation.

There was confusion and some denial in Tina's story as well. Tina's mother was able to tell Tina of her aunt's AIDS, but she did not tell her that she too had AIDS. Instead the mother relied on the aunt to tell Tina of her diagnosis. Because of the secrecy surrounding the disclosure of her aunt's illness, Tina feigned ignorance when her aunt told her about her mother. It appears that after her aunt told her, neither Tina nor her mother brought up the subject with each other for several months. Then, even though she had brought up the subject with her sisters within earshot of her mother, Tina pretended not to know. Instead she wanted her mother to tell her directly about her illness.

Joe told me that when his mother was in jail she began to talk to him about her illness. However, it was not until she was released from jail that Joe realized that she had AIDS. It is not clear where the communication break-down occurred, whether Joe was not able to take in the information or his mother did not tell him clearly. Either way, this again confirms how difficult the disclosure of a parent's AIDS can be.

The three participants had varying reactions to the stigma surrounding AIDS. Joe told me he did not talk much about his mother because of the pain involved, but he was appreciative of any support people gave him. Maria was characteristically belligerent in her approach to the subject. She told me that she didn't care if people knew that her parents had died of AIDS, but she was very selective in whom she told. Tina told no one but a former neighbor, whose own mother had died of AIDS and with whom she had only intermittent contact. She appeared to suffer greatly in Sex Education class, ruminating on her own situation and despising her classmates, whom she imagined would revile her as infectious if they knew about her mother's illness. She voiced concern over the all too common perception that family members of people with AIDS may themselves have the disease. For adolescents and young adults the real or imagined possibility of rejection by peers because of fear and ignorance about their parent's illness can be especially isolating and painful.

RESPONDING TO AIDS AFFECTED YOUTH

Both the findings of this study and the literature point to the fact that adolescents and young adults affected by AIDS may be reacting to the crisis in their families in ways which make them very difficult to work with. Inaccessibility, anger, and behavior problems are some of the factors which can complicate the tasks of identifying and meeting the needs of these young people. The following is an anecdote which illustrates some of the problems of teens affected by a mother's AIDS and an all too typical response to them.

Johnny's Story

Johnny was a student in my school who was chronically truant. He came to the Sex Education teacher's attention after an angry outburst in class during a lesson on AIDS. He had refused to answer a question, and instead began cursing, telling the other students that they didn't know anything about AIDS. She spoke with him privately after class, and he told her he felt that "no one can understand" what he was going through. When she realized that his mother was sick and surmised it was from AIDS, she confided in him that she had lost her mother as a teenager. He then told her that his mother had AIDS. Unfortunately, he did not come back to school again for the rest of the term.

I met Johnny when he came back to school during the summer session. I had been told he needed counseling because of his truancy and his frequent fights when he did come to school. Johnny told me he did not want to be seen in group counseling because he did not want to talk in front of other students. I honored his request and saw him individually. He began talking about the "beef" or serious problems he was having with a gang around his grandmother's house. It had become impossible for him to live there because he feared he would be jumped and beaten up. As I explored his living situation with him it was clear that he had been moving around a lot in the past year, living with various relatives. Although I didn't know his mother was ill, the pattern of shifting from one relative to another was familiar to me from the stories of the AIDS affected teenagers I had spoken to for this study. I gently explored this with him, and he sadly told me that his mother had AIDS.

Johnny's attendance was spotty during the final four weeks of the summer session. At one point he was out of school for a week. When he returned he showed me bruises on his face and told me he had been arrested for arguing with the police about a summons for public drinking. He said he had been beaten at the station house. I suggested he file a complaint, and although he said his father was going to, they did not follow up.

In those four weeks his living situation changed twice. He moved out of his grandmother's house after a fight during which he threatened his uncle with a knife. He moved to another uncle's house, and two weeks later moved to his father's house. He had been estranged from his father for several years, but he was hopeful the new living arrangement would work out. However, he soon told me that his father was moving down to Florida for several months, and he would stay with his father's girlfriend. Shortly after that, he abruptly stopped coming to school again, and although I tried, I could not reach him.

I did not see Johnny again until several weeks after the Fall school term began. We spoke briefly, and he agreed to come to my office to resume counseling the next day. I was dismayed, but not entirely surprised, when he failed to show up. After several days of calling his teachers to find out if he had come in I learned that he had been suspended for fighting with another student and that he had been told not to come back to school without his mother, with whom he was again living. I told the administration that Johnny's mother was very ill and might not be able to make it in, and it was agreed that Johnny could return without her. I called the house and spoke to his mother, who promised to come in the following week. I told her I was looking forward to meeting her, but that if she were not able to come in on the appointed day Johnny could come in without her. She asked discreetly if I knew that she was sick, and I said that I understood that she was. She did not say what was the matter with her, nor did I, but she said that her illness was hard on Johnny. I agreed and told her I wanted to work together with them to help him cope. The following week neither Johnny nor his mother showed up, and there was no answer when I called them. I continued to try for the next week and a half with no luck.

I then discovered that Johnny and his father had visited the school to gain his readmission. However, instead of seeing me or a member of the administration they had spoken first with a teacher. I went to him and asked about Johnny. He told me, with a great deal of contempt in his voice, how he had spoken to Johnny and told him simply to stay home for the next few days and think about whether he really wanted to come to our school. If he felt he could follow the rules he could return the following week, but if not he should not bother to come back.

I told the teacher that Johnny was going through a lot of stress and that he needed support and should be in school. He replied that Johnny's father had told him that the mother was sick, but that "they don't have a clue" about what was the matter with her. I gave him a very significant look and said that, yes, his mother was <u>very</u> sick and that her illness was seriously affecting Johnny. I thought the teacher might understand and realize what was going on, but he didn't. He said derisively that he didn't know what was "with these people" but that the mother was in the hospital, "probably with some kind of cancer" and the family "didn't have a clue" about what was happening with her.

I was thoroughly disgusted. I told him I was going to call Johnny. He informed me that the father had no phone and the phone and address on record were those of the mother. Since she was in the hospital it would be impossible to reach them. He then said, "Do me a favor, and don't even try to call him. Even if he does come back he's just going to be trouble. He'll be here for a few days and then out for a few weeks, just like before."

I felt speechless with anger at his arrogance and insensitivity. However, I did not want to tell him what was really going on, and I understood why Johnny and his father had not told him either. Not surprisingly, Johnny never returned to school, and despite my efforts I was never able to contact him. His mother's phone was disconnected a few weeks later. I felt sad and very angry at the teacher. How dare he misuse his position to push away a needy youngster because he was too troublesome to deal with? I felt that his certainty that he was better than Johnny and his father is what kept them from telling him the truth and kept him from recognizing it.

I felt angry at myself too. Johnny had opened up to me, but why couldn't I have engaged him and helped him to reconnect with the school? Maybe the evidence from his experience that no one understands was just too overwhelming to refute. Maybe the pain was just too great. Maybe there was just no precedent in his life for connecting for too long.

It's very easy to lay the blame on the teacher, and surely he did deserve some of it for his arrogance and insensitivity in pushing Johnny away. But the problem is far deeper than that. Even when people in helping positions are sensitive and trying to connect, they often still fail to engage many of the teenagers affected by AIDS. In conversations over the past six years some of these genuine helpers have told me that it's very difficult to get many of these teens into counseling and even more difficult to keep them coming (personal communications with: A. Simmons, Social Worker Mt. Sinai Adolescent Health Center, February 28, 1991; Nurse, Montefiore Adolescent AIDS Center, January 21, 1993; M. Riedel, Social Worker, Columbia Presbyterian Adolescent AIDS Program, September 7, 1995; L. Schnee, Health Educator, Mt. Sinai Adolescent Health Center, November 13, 1995).

IMPLICATIONS

Schools

I believe that there are important implications for schools stemming from this study. Schools can provide stability and a site for delivery of services for AIDS affected young people. School staff need to be educated to recognize the behaviors exhibited by many AIDS affected youngsters and to develop services targeted to meet their specific needs, rather than subsuming them into generic special education referrals.

Amidst the wrenching family crisis and changes in living arrangements, schools can provide an anchor of stability in the lives of AIDS affected youngsters. Teenagers and young adults, unlike younger students, can usually continue to attend their old school even after moving some distance from their former neighborhood. This can provide a reassuring sense of continuity in both their education and their friends to offset the disorienting changes and loss in other areas of their lives. Teachers especially, by virtue of their daily contact with young people, can play an important role in maintaining stable, caring adult relationships. AIDS affected youth can greatly benefit from the attention and understanding of sensitive teachers who are able to see beyond and manage their acting out, listen with compassion and respect for the young person's confidentiality, and provide appropriate referrals. In addition to emotional support, young people affected by AIDS may need extra help with schoolwork because of the strain their current situation places on their mental resources and/or their possible longstanding academic difficulties.

School may be the best place to locate services such as counseling for AIDS affected students who attend with some regularity. Attendance at community based counseling services can be compromised by the parent's illness and other demands. Even if the young people are able to go to counseling appointments alone, they may choose not to make a special trip. The newer "one stop shopping" AIDS clinics (Mellins, 1995) where medical, mental health and social services for people with AIDS are located in one site may be convenient for the ill parent, but they may not be a suitable venue for counseling older children. Teenagers and young adults may not choose to accompany their parents to these clinics, especially if they are estranged. If a student is attending school, this seems to be the most accessible place to locate services. Schools must rise to this challenge by educating teachers and counselors about the needs of AIDS affected young people and how best to help them. Issues such as behavior problems, confidentiality and accessing social services will need to be addressed.

The behavior problems frequently manifested by AIDS affected young people can cause great concern and negative reactions in school staff. Teachers and counselors may not understand the troublesome and at times aggressive behavior these adolescents may exhibit. Absenteeism, academic difficulties and disruptive behavior may be related to the young person's upset and grief at the illness and death of a parent from AIDS. There is a need for more open-ended forms of addressing behavior problems than automatic referrals to more restrictive educational environments. The move to a new program which these referrals often precipitate can exacerbate the problem by depriving youngsters of what may be one of the few sources of stability and continuity in their lives. Behavior management consultation for teachers and in-school mental health services for affected youngsters may be sufficient to address behavior problems in the classroom and preclude a move to a new program.

Teachers, attendance personnel, and counselors need to be sensitive to the fact that excessive absences and frequent changes of address can be a sign that a youngster may be affected by AIDS in the family. Young people who do not attend school are often the most vulnerable. Every attempt should be made to reach out, engage them and provide support and appropriate referrals for the young people and their families.

Sexuality Education

Literature on HIV prevention with adolescents is extensive and beyond the scope of this study. I will limit my comments to those implications which relate specifically to the situation of AIDS affected youngsters. The alienation and isolation that these young people feel need to be addressed, especially when AIDS is being discussed. Teachers of Sexuality Education and other subjects need to be sensitized to the fact that they are likely to have some students affected by AIDS in their class, especially if they are teaching in an economically deprived area. A form of mental health universal precautions should be adopted, similar to those used by medical personnel. Because we usually do not know who is affected and who is not, it is best to assume that at least some students in the class are.

One practical step in helping AIDS affected youth is to "normalize" the situation by acknowledging the fact that there are many youngsters in this predicament. It could be beneficial to discuss living with persons with AIDS and the needs of AIDS affected families, especially children and youth, as long as students' confidentiality is not compromised.

HIV prevention is never a simple matter of increasing knowledge of risks, such as intravenous drug use, and safer sex behaviors. This is especially true for AIDS affected young people. Interventions should have a holistic approach, with priority given to addressing the issues of unstable housing and bereavement which affect these youngsters. Sexuality Education instruction itself should not focus on fear arousal, as AIDS affected youth may be feeling particularly anxious, and this can be immobilizing. Rather students should be taught to realistically appraise risks and should be exposed to situations where their competence in problem solving can be developed, experienced and acknowledged. Role playing and other action-oriented formats can be particularly useful in engaging youth, as well as in providing opportunities to practice skills. Needs for affiliation and pleasure should be addressed, as unsafe sex is too often the medium by which these needs are satisfied. For those young people who already have babies, parenting education may be most useful.

Counseling

Given that this study is based on a small number of AIDS affected young people, if the results are indicative of other AIDS affected youth, there are several lessons that may be drawn from the experiences of the participants of this study that seem relevant to counseling AIDS affected youth. As a precondition to working with clients, many mental health professionals require that they demonstrate motivation and commitment by maintaining good attendance at sessions. AIDS affected young people, given their tenuous living situations and their difficulty with limits may need a more active approach, with outreach from mental health professionals seeking to work with them. They may not believe in the counselor's commitment or reliability, or they may be so overwhelmed with the instability of their own lives that they may need helping adults to take the initiative in making and sustaining contact, especially in the early stages of the work. Geballe et al. and Hollander (1995) recommend that mental health professionals make home visits to bring services to AIDS affected families. Even when this is not possible, counselors may need to adopt a more active, outreach approach than usual in their work.

There are conflicting views among mental health professionals as to whether parents suffering from AIDS should disclose their diagnosis to their children (Levine & Stein). Some feel this should be strongly encouraged, others support disclosure but don't encourage it, and still others feel it should be left entirely to the parent's discretion. Studies show that the majority of parents with AIDS do not tell their children of their diagnosis (Bettoli-Vaughn; Nagler, Adnopoz & Forsyth; Rotheram-Borus, 1995). It may be damaging for parents to withhold information on their diagnosis, as Maria's story illustrates. However, counselors must realize that there are good reasons for parents not to tell their children that they have AIDS. Parents with AIDS have to be able to accept or at least acknowledge their impending death in order to disclose their condition to their children and plan for custody after their death. Even though protease inhibitors currently offer the promise of reducing the death rate from AIDS, they do not work for everyone. Furthermore, doctors do not prescribe them for actively using drug addicts and others whose life style they judge will seriously interfere with compliance with the demanding regimen (Sontag & Richardson, 1997).

Another factor is that if parents do disclose, their children will have to keep the information secret because of the fear that public disclosure might subject the family to rejection and discrimination from neighbors, landlords, employers, insurance companies, and even medical personnel. I think that disclosure should be encouraged, but its implications and the ability of individual family members to cope with the information must be thought through. Since the literature points to the fact that teenagers do worst when disclosure is not accompanied by plans for their care after the parent's death (Rotheram-Borus, 1995), these must be seen as an integral part of any plan for disclosure.

Two primary issues which need to be addressed by counselors of AIDS affected youth are resolving the question of where and how they will live and grieving the loss of their parent. Even though they may be in their late teens, some AIDS affected youth may not be ready to live independently. When this is the case, the problem of finding a place to live and adults to watch over them until they are ready to move out on their own is a survival issue and needs to be addressed first. If extended family members or other adults are willing to take them in they may need support to understand and cope with the often distressing behavior problems and resistance to authority which AIDS affected young people may manifest. If family or foster care are not available, then group settings need to be considered. Whatever arrangements are made, they should provide emotional support and structure while helping the young people to address and work through issues of independence and their relationship to authority.

The issue of grieving is complex for AIDS affected young people. Like other youngsters who have lost a parent, they must come to terms with and mourn their loss. However, the circumstances of their lives and the ramifications of a diagnosis of AIDS can greatly complicate these tasks. For one thing, the death of their parent is often not their only loss, and their grief can be compounded by the propensity for this most recent tragedy to resurrect the pain of previous losses. More specific to AIDS, the stigma of the disease greatly magnifies the anguish of the loss and often impedes disclosure and discussion. I think it is important to try to erode the stigma of AIDS in the family by talking about it in an open but non-intrusive manner and "normalizing" it by stressing how common it is. Nevertheless, it has often been my experience that AIDS affected young people do not want to be seen in a group, even with other AIDS affected peers. They often prefer individual counseling to enable them to disclose and work through the many problems they are struggling with. They should have access to individual counseling sessions and have the choice of continuing with individual sessions or using them as a prelude or adjunct to group counseling sessions. AIDS affected young people have a great deal to offer each other in terms of empathy and support, but they should not be forced to attend group counseling or to disclose in a group setting before they are ready.

Other factors which may complicate grieving for many AIDS affected youth can include the effects of racism, poverty, substance abuse, family disintegration, and violence in the home and community. These issues are similar for many young people in poor, urban communities, but they are both exacerbated by and exacerbate the problems brought on by AIDS in the family.

It is important to keep in mind that AIDS affected young people may have intense and ambivalent feelings towards their ailing or deceased parents. This can include anger at possible past neglect or abuse or at the parent's drug use, especially if that is how they became infected with HIV. They may feel some guilt, such as Tina expressed after her mother's suicide attempt. Counselors need to help young people to explore these issues and to assess them realistically. Sometimes family members may reinforce guilt by suggesting that the youth's bad behavior hastened the parent's death or that the parent is watching him/her misbehave from heaven. Counselors can help by not reinforcing this guilt. If it is not addressed, the guilt engendered by the young person's ambivalence or the admonitions of others can interfere with mourning and contribute to symptoms of antisocial behavior, where the aim is to be caught and punished (Dane & Miller).

Commemoration of Loss

The formal commemoration of loss can help mourners to find meaning and cope with the pain of the death of a loved one. Religious rituals for the dead and funerals both seek to do this. The arts can also play a vital role in commemorating loss by externalizing and giving distance and perspective to intense feelings and by creating a product that lends substance and grace to one's experience. Artistic creations can also be shared with others so that the experience of the creators can be acknowledged, and they can receive understanding and support. Participants who share similar experiences may gain insight and feel affirmed through the experience of the art work.

Goldstein remarked on the role of the arts in helping the gay community to bear witness to their experience of the AIDS epidemic and to express grief and promote solidarity. However, he felt that,

> No comparable process of self expression exists among the other groups hit hardest by AIDS-IV drug users, their children, and their mostly black or Hispanic partners-in part because there is no "community" perceived as such, to bind drug users together (Dane and Miller, p. 8).

Dane and Miller suggest a,

> potential to build on the existing cultural and religious heritage to create meaningful modes of expression that allow children to feel not only their loss

but also the support of their own community and, ultimately, the larger community as well (Ibid.).

Rituals such as Tina's lighting of candles, which derives from Hispanic religious practice, can prove an intimate and comforting way to commemorate loved ones who have died of AIDS. Counselors of AIDS affected youth can assist the young people to create traditional or original means to memorialize their dead. They may be private and intimate, like Tina's candles, or group efforts. On the group level, even reticent youngsters who cannot yet tell their own stories can relieve the isolation so often felt by AIDS affected youth and find comfort and understanding through participating in or even just witnessing the work of others.

It is important that whatever memorial is created represents the genuine expressions of AIDS affected participants. Although helping adults may wish to emphasize the positive aspects of the deceased, perhaps for their own comfort, they should resist any impulse to whitewash the youths' expression. They need to realize that the experience of many AIDS affected youth may include issues of drugs, dislocation, neglect, sexuality, and abuse. These issues, along with positive feelings for the parent, are valid, integral parts of many youngsters' stories and must be heard and attended to. Appendix A shows an example of a memorial created by a group of AIDS affected adolescents reflecting their unique, authentic expressions of their experience.

APPLICATION OF FINDINGS

Writing this dissertation has helped me in my practice as a school psychologist working in an area with a high incidence of AIDS in several ways.

On a clinical level, I'm able to recognize some signs associated with AIDS in a student's family sooner and more easily. This can enable me to facilitate their disclosure. The anecdote about Johnny provides an example of this. Given the fact that in my experience students do not readily disclose this information, this clue has enabled me to address the issue of AIDS far sooner than previously.

The knowledge I've gained from this study has also influenced my work with a theater group which I run at my school. Besides the usual AIDS prevention work, which many teen theater groups do, our theater group has focused on needs of teens affected by AIDS. In the spring of 1996 we completed a "novela" or Spanish soap opera video about a group of teenagers whose lives are affected by HIV and AIDS in various ways. At the end of the video the audience discovers that the lead character's mother is sick with AIDS. He delivers a soliloquy on whether he should tell his girlfriend or continue to hide it. This question was purposely left open-ended for audience discussion after showing the video. We made two videos, one in English and the other in

Spanish, so as not to exclude the Spanish language dominant students in our school.

The Multimedia AIDS Quilt

The most profound effect that this study has had on my clinical work to date took shape last spring in the Multimedia AIDS Quilt group. I originally proposed the quilt group as a way to memorialize family members whom students in the school had lost to AIDS. I put together a small steering committee of several students who had collaborated with me in the theater group and on other projects. I originally proposed that our group could participate in the National AIDS Quilt by sewing a cloth panel, as other high schools were doing. Some students did not like that idea, and one loudly protested that he did not want to sew and, "You know no one in this school is going to sit down and sew anything." I had to agree with him, and I proposed instead that we use a computer to create a virtual quilt.

Instead of sewing panels we used a multimedia computer program to assemble drawings, photographs and video clips about AIDS into a quilt pattern on the first page of the presentation. Viewers can click on any panel in order to see it enlarged and hear a voice-over first person narrative telling the story of a student who was affected by AIDS through the illness or death of a family member. The point of the project was to provide a forum for affected students to tell their stories so they could support and learn from each other.

We recruited more students for the group and began our project. The criteria for participants was only that they respect the privacy of anyone who might want to contribute to the project and be open and sensitive to their concerns. Of the seven original members of the group, only one young man had previously disclosed to me the loss of a family member from AIDS. In the first few weeks of the project, four more group members privately disclosed to me that they were affected by AIDS in their families. One of these had lost a father, and his estranged mother was living with AIDS. Another had lost both parents to AIDS. At first neither of these teens wanted the other group members to know, nor did a third group member whose mother was living with AIDS. Two other students had lost aunts to AIDS. One of these spoke out in group, and the other said he wanted to, but took several months to do so. I did not push any of these young people to disclose, and I believe it was therapeutic for them to listen to other group members without being coerced into telling their own story before they were ready.

At the time I was working with the Multimedia AIDS Quilt group, I had just put my dissertation participants' words into free verse, and I was particularly struck by Tina's words about lighting a candle. It offered an accessible and private way to commemorate her loss and work through her grief. She had returned from California and was calling me every few months, just to say hello. I asked her if we could use her words for the quilt, and she enthusiastically gave her permission. I told her that her statement would be anonymous, but after calling me several times to discuss it, she asked to visit the Multimedia AIDS Quilt group. She came to our meeting, and for the first time in public she disclosed that her mother had died of AIDS. She seemed to relish the attention from the other group members, even as she told them how difficult it had been for her to cope with her mother's death.

After Tina's visit, I interviewed several of the AIDS affected group members, as well as other affected students from outside the group. All interviews were conducted in private and lasted about thirty minutes. I asked them who in their family had died of AIDS and to tell me about that person. I transcribed their words, put them into free verse and edited for accessibility, continuity, and length. I went over the pieces with each of the students to determine if they faithfully represented their experiences. Students were somewhat awed by the fact that their words were now poetry. I felt that this provided them with some distance on their experience and gave a formal recognition of the importance of their story.

A sample of some of their stories from the Multimedia AIDS Quilt "panels" are found in Appendix A. They reflect many of the themes found in the study participants' stories, such as family conflict, dislocation, drug use, and loss.

Excerpts from the Multimedia AIDS Quilt

MY PARENTS

When I was about 13 years old.
My mom sat down and told me she had AIDS.
I didn't know what that was.
I just felt sad.
I didn't know what was going on.
I took the word
AIDS
But I didn't know what it meant.
They didn't talk about it in the school I went to.
Until I came to this school,
Then I learned about AIDS.
And then I knew.
I was wondering why she was getting so skinny.
She used to be chubby,
Then her face started sinking in.
I always wondered why.
Now I know what it was.
I loved my mother.
I had a big problem with my stepdad,
So I had to leave and come live with my grandma.
When I first left
I used to cry every night.
I was depending on my mother.
How could I say it?

I was depending on her
So she could live to see me when I was older.
But she died last year.
I knew my dad died a long time ago
I just heard he died of the same thing.
I got a lot of people in my family
That died of AIDS.
It's sad.
I don't know what it is.
The world is crazy.
When my mom said she was dying,
I couldn't believe it.
I used to tell her she was gonna live,
Cause I didn't want to lose her.
I already had lost my father.
And now I guess I have nobody.

DAD

My Dad died of AIDS in 1990.
He looked weird,
I didn't recognize him.
When he was healthy
He looked like me.
Before he got sick
We didn't live with him
We had to live with my grandmother.
Every New Years I'd be thinking
He was gonna come back
Another New Years to start over
I wanted the whole family to be together
Mother, Dad, brother, sister
Like a normal family.
I think about all the things
We should've done
When he was alive.
If I would've known he was gonna die,
I'da been with him,
Doing whatever a father and son does.
At the end he couldn't move.
He stayed with us in my grandma's house
Until he got really bad.

Then he went to the hospital.
He died the next day.
He was real skinny.
I thought he was just sick.
My grandmother told me and my brother
My Dad was doing bad things,
Hanging out with bad people,
Doing drugs.
That's how he got AIDS.
That was stupid.
I'm a little mad.
Not all that mad,
I forgive him.
But I feel a little anger inside me,
Cause he was using drugs.
When my grandmother die
Then who we gonna have?

LIVING WITH AIDS

My mother is living with AIDS.
For me it's hard to live with her.
She gets angry sometimes.
We argue,
And sometimes I don't keep my mouth quiet.
I talk back.
I'm scared.
If she has sex with a person
Without a condom
She could get more sick.
My sister and me yell at her
To take better care of herself.
I worry about her,
But she don't know.
She thinks I don't love her.
She gets stressed out and blames things on me.
I think she's taking her anger out on me.
I can't take it any more.
That's why I'm planning to move.

MY AUNT

My aunt died from AIDS 6 years ago.
We were close.
I always used to stay with her.
It was hard when I lost her.
She died cause
She was sleeping around
And not protecting herself.
My mother told her to slow down with guys
And protect herself.
But she never listened.
She stayed with us when she got sick.
When I found out she had AIDS
I was scared.
I thought I was gonna catch it.
I took counseling
And they told me
I wouldn't catch it
Drinking from her glass.
She got skinny
And she was going crazy in her mind.
She looked so different.
You used to talk to her,
And she would just laugh.
She used to talk to herself.
She used to take a lot of pills.
Not a little.
A lot.
When she went to the hospital
She was on a machine.
The machine made her fat.
It was sad.
The family, her father and them
Wouldn't accept she had AIDS.
He wouldn't come to see her.
"That's not my daughter!" he said.
When she died he didn't come to the funeral.
I loved her a lot.
She was my favorite aunt
Cause, after my mother,

She was always there for me.
She used to talk to me.
She was nice.
She left three kids behind.
They're living with us now.

MY FAVORITE AUNT

My aunt had the virus.
She got it doing sexual activity.
She didn't know from who.
She was smoking crack.
She was a cool person.
She was nice to me.
It's always gonna be inside my mind, the way she told me,
"Me and you never had secrets."
I said, "What's wrong?"
She said, "I have to tell you this.
I got AIDS."
I started to cry.
She was real sad.
She told me she was gonna
Kill herself.
I told her,
"God gave you life.
God gave you everything you need."
She said she knew,
And she went back to church again.
Then 2 or 3 months later
She went back to drugs.
Drugs, drugs, drugs, drugs, drugs.
She stole her mother's jewelry and tv.
She got more sick.
They took her to Lincoln Hospital,
And the doctor told us
There's nothing to do about it because
The virus is too strong.
She couldn't even get up.
The virus was eating her inside.
She was going house, hospital,
House, hospital, house, hospital.
The doctor said, "It's over.

We have to take the medicine off."
She was real sick,
But she was not drinking the medicine.
She would put it in her sock.
She went back home again.
She told me, "I'm gonna miss you."
I said, "Why you say that?
You gonna be alright!"
She said, "Tell my husband to come
And bring my dog."
He came and gave her a kiss,
And the dog licked her,
And she died.
That was her favorite dog.

MY UNCLE

My uncle died from AIDS
He was in jail.
My parents wouldn't talk to him
Because he did some bad things
Before he went to jail.
But he was nice to me.
He used to spoil me,
Buy me anything,
Take me anyplace.
He went to jail when I was about seven.
I felt like I lost my best friend.
He wrote a letter to me
From jail.
He told me he had AIDS,
And he still wanted me to write to him,
And to be there for him.
When he died
They called my house.
My mother wasn't home,
So I answered.
When they told me,
I felt very sad

Statement to the Participants

I am interested in interviewing young people who have family members who have AIDS or who have died from the disease. I want to find out how they think having a relative with the disease has affected them. I believe that the best way to learn what this is like is from the people who are going through it.

If you agree to participate we will meet several times (probably about three) to talk for an hour or two each time. I have just a few specific questions to start with. Most of the time I'll be interested in hearing your opinions and what you think is important about the topic. I will audiotape our conversations so that I can remember what was said.

I will not let anyone else listen to the tapes, but you can listen to whatever parts of them you want to with me. I will keep the tapes in a locked drawer in my apartment. I will not use your real name or identify you in any way in my work.

You have the right to stop participating in this study at any time and for any reason. Nothing will be held against you if you decide you no longer want to participate, and I will not use our conversations in the study. You can also tell me to take out any part of our conversations you don't feel comfortable about.

Lists of Categories for Each Participant

CATEGORIES IN MARIA INTERVIEWS 1&2

Doc/Memo (Doc= coded document completed; Memo=Analytic memo done)
ABUSEK: Abusive behavior by participant
ABUSEPAR: Abusive behavior by parents
AIDSMOT
AIDSYMP: Symptoms of AIDS & their effects
ALONE: Participant's feelings of loss & aloneness
ANGERK: Anger of participant
ANGERMOT: Mother's anger
BABY: Participant's knowledge and feelings about baby
DEATH: Participant's thoughts and feelings about death
DEATHFAT: Death of father
DEATHMOT: Death of mother
DEPRK: Symptoms of depression in participant
DISCFAM: Disclosure of AIDS & the family (combined w/ Secrecy)
DISCFAT: Father's disclosure of AIDS
DISCMOT: Mother's (non)disclosure of AIDS
DRUGSK: Drug use by participant
DRUGSPAR: Drug use by parents
EDU: Participant's thoughts on education (Combined w/ School)
FAM: Participant's family
FEARPWA: Fear on part of person with AIDS
GENDER: Participant's thoughts on gender roles
HEALTHK: Health of participant
IDPAR: Identification with parents
JEAL: Participant's jealousy
KNOWAIDS: Participant's knowledge of AIDS

LIVING: Participant's living arrangements
MOT: Description of mother
MOTPREG: Reaction of mother to partic's pregnancy
MOVE: Changes in participant's living situation
OPPSEX: Participant's relationship w/ other sex
PREG: Pregnancy of participant
RELATMOT: Participant's relationship w/ mother
SAD: Sadness of participant
SCHOOL: Events in school
SECY: Secrecy, especially around AIDS
SELFREL: Self reliance by participant
SFSX: Safe sex knowledge & practices by participant
SIB: Participant's siblings
SUPPORT: Participant's support network
SELF IMAGE
ENVIRONMENT

CATEGORIES IN JOE INTERVIEWS 1&2

Doc/Memo
ABUSEK: Abusive behavior by participant
ABUSEPAR: Abusive behavior by parents or guardians
##ACTOUT: Acting out behavior by participant
AIDSK
AIDSYMP: Symptoms of AIDS & their effects
ALONE: Participant's feelings of loss and aloneness
ANGERK: Anger of participant
ANGERMOT: Mother's anger
##ANX: Participant's anxiety
BABY: Participant's knowledge and feelings about baby
DEATH: Participant's thoughts and feelings about death
DEATHFAT: Death of father
DEATHMOT: Death of mother
DEPRK: Symptoms of depression in participant
##DISAB: Participant's disability
DISCFAM: Disclosure of AIDS & the family
DISCFAT: Father's disclosure of AIDS
DISCMOT: Mother's (non)disclosure of AIDS
DRUGSK: Drug use by participant
DRUGSPAR: Drug use by parents
EDU: Participant's thoughts on education
FAM: Participant's family

FEARPWA: Fear on part of person with AIDS
##FUTURE: Participant's thoughts & wishes re: future
GENDER: Participant's thoughts on gender roles
HEALTHK: Health of participant
IDPAR: Identification with parents
##JAILMOT: Mother's criminal behavior &/or jail time
JEAL: Participant's jealousy
KNOWAIDS: Participant's knowledge of AIDS
LIVING: Participant's living arrangements
MOT: Description of mother
MOTPREG: Reaction of mother to partic's pregnancy
MOVE: Changes in participant's living situation
OPPSEX: Participant's relationship with other sex
PARNTG: @@Participant's parenting behaviors & ideas
PREG: Pregnancy of participant
RELATMOT: Participant's relationship with mother
SAD: Sadness of participant
SCHOOL: Events in school
SECY: Secrecy, especially around AIDS
SELFIM: Participant's self image
SELFREL: Self reliance by participant
SFSX: Safe sex knowledge and practices by participant
SIB: Participant's siblings
SICK: ##Participant's illness
SOCSERV: ##Social services
SUPPORT: Participant's support network
UNREL: ##Unreliability on part of participants
WORK: Work (legal & illegal) of participant
SXTYMOT: ## Mother's sexuality
COPING
COUNSELING
New Codes: Tina(@@) or (##) Joe. Look for in other participants

CATEGORIES IN TINA INTERVIEWS 1, 2 & 3

Doc/Memo
ABUSEK: Abusive behavior by participant
ABUSEPAR: Abusive behavior by parents
AIDSK
AIDSMOT
AIDSYMP: Symptoms of AIDS & their effects
ALONE: Participant's feelings of loss and aloneness

ANGERK: Anger of participant
ANGERMOT: Mother's anger
BABY: Participant's knowledge and feelings about baby
BELIEF: @@Participant's beliefs & sense made of events
CAUSE: @@Of parent's AIDS
CNSG: @@Counseling
COPING: @@Mechanisms used
DEATH: Participant's thoughts and feelings about death
DEATHFAM: @@Other deaths in participant's family
DEATHFAT: Death of father
DEATHMOT: Death of mother
DEPRK: Symptoms of depression in participant
DISCFAM: Disclosure of AIDS & the family
DISCFAT: Father's disclosure of AIDS
DISCMOT: Mother's (non)disclosure of AIDS
DRUGSK: Drug use by participant
DRUGSPAR: Drug use by parents
EDU: Participant's thoughts on education
FAM: Participant's family
FEARPWA: Fear on part of person with AIDS
FUNERAL: @@Parent's funeral
GENDER: Participant's thoughts on gender roles
HEALTHK: Health of participant
IDPAR: Identification with parents
JEAL: Participant's jealousy
KNOWAIDS: Participant's knowledge of AIDS
LIVING: Participant's living arrangements
MOT: Description of mother
MOTPREG: Reaction of mother to partic's pregnancy
MOVE: Changes in participant's living situation
OPPSEX: Participant's relationship with other sex
PARNTG: @@Participant's parenting behaviors & ideas
PREG: Pregnancy of participant
RELATMOT: Participant's relationship with mother
SAD: Sadness of participant
SCHOOL: Events in school
SECY: Secrecy, especially around AIDS
SELFREL: Self reliance by participant
SFSX: Safe sex knowledge and practices by participant
SIB: Participant's siblings
SOCSERV: ##Social services

SUIC: @@Suicide
SUPPORT: Participant's support network
UNREL: ##Unreliability on part of participants
New Codes: Tina(@@) or (##) Joe. Look for in other participants

Bibliography

Altman, L. (1999, December 2). U.N. issues grim report on the 11 million children orphaned by AIDS. *New York Times*, p. A12.

Atkinson, P. (1992). *Understanding ethnographic texts*. Newbury Park, CA: Sage Publications.

Bandura, A. (1986). Self-efficacy mechanism in human agency. *American Psychologist, 37*, 122–147.

Bandura, A. (1989). Perceived self-efficacy in the exercise of control over AIDS infection. In Mays, V., Albee, G. & Schneider, S. *Primary prevention of AIDS* (pp. 128–141). Newbury Park, CA: Sage Publications.

Barth, R., Pietrzak, J., & Ramler, M. (Eds.). (1993). *Families living with drugs and HIV: Intervention and treatment strategies*. New York: Guilford Press.

Bettoli-Vaughn, E. (1995, August). *Adaptation of siblings of children with AIDS and their mothers*. Poster session presented at the annual meeting of the American Psychological Association, New York, NY.

Biddle, G. (1992). *Alphabet City*. Berkeley: University of California Press.

Bogdan, R. & Bicklen, S. (1982). *Qualitative research for education: An introduction to theory and methods*. Boston: Allyn & Bacon.

Britton, P., de Mauro, D. & Gambrell, A. (1992). HIV/AIDS Education. *SIECUS Report, 21* (1), 1–8.

Brooklyn Legal Services Corp. B. and Gay Men's Health Crisis. (undated) *Facing the future: A legal handbook for parents with HIV disease*.

Brooks-Gunn, J., Boyer, C. & Hein, K. (1988). Preventing HIV infection and AIDS in children and adolescents. *American Psychologist. 43*, 958–964.

Brown, L. & Fritz, G. (1988). AIDS education in the schools: A literature review as a guide for curriculum planning. *Clinical pediatrics, 27* (7), 311–316.

Brown, L., Fritz, G. & Barone, V. (1989). The impact of AIDS education on junior and senior high school students. *Journal of adolescent health care, 10*, 386–392.

Centers for Disease Control [CDC]. (1992a). Mortality Patterns-United States, 1989. *Morbidity and mortality weekly report [MMWR], 41* (7), 121–125.

CDC. (1992b). HIV instruction and selected HIV-risk behaviors among high school students-United States, 1989–1991. *MMWR, 41* (46), 866–868.

CDC. (1992c). Selected behaviors that increase risk for HIV infection, other sexually transmitted diseases, and unintended pregnancy among high school students-United States, 1991. *MMWR, 41* (50), 945–951.

CDC. (1992d). Revised classification system for HIV infection and expanded surveillance case definition for AIDS among adolescents and adults. *MMWR, 41* (RR-17), 1–13.

CDC. (1993). Impact of the expanded AIDS surveillance case definition on AIDS case reporting-United States, first quarter, 1993. *MMWR, 42* (16), 308–310.

CDC. (1996). Clinical update: Impact of HIV protease inhibitors on the treatment of HIV-infected tuberculosis patients with rifampin. *MMWR, 45* (42), 921.

CDC. (1997a). Update: Trends in AIDS incidence, deaths, and prevalence-United States, 1996. *MMWR, 46* (8), 165–173.

CDC. (1997b). *HIV/AIDS semi-annual surveillance report. 9* (1).

CDC. (1999). Basic statistics, [online]. (Division of AIDS Prevention). www.cdc.gov/nchstp/hiv_aids/stats/cumulati.htm. [1/29/00]

Chachkes, E. & Jennings, R. (1994). Latino communities: Coping with death. In Dane, B. & Levine, C. (Eds.). *AIDS and the new orphans: Coping with death* (pp. 77–100). Westport, CT: Auburn House.

Cohen, F. (1993). Epidemiology of HIV infection and AIDS in women. In Durham, J. & Cohen, F. (Eds.). *Women, children and HIV/AIDS* (pp. 43–59). New York: Springer.

Cotton, D. & Watts, D.H. (Eds.). (1997). *The medical management of AIDS in women.* New York: Wiley-Liss.

Crenshaw, D. (1990). Bereavement: Counseling the grieving throughout the life cycle. New York: Continuum.

Dane, B. (1994). Death and bereavement. In Dane, B. & Levine, C. (Eds.). *AIDS and the new orphans: Coping with death* (pp. 13–32). Westport, CT: Auburn House.

Dane, B., & Miller, S. (1992). *AIDS: Intervening with hidden grievers.* Westport, Ct: Auburn House.

Demb, J. (1989). Clinical vignette: Adolescent "survivors" of parents with AIDS. *Family Systems Medicine, 7* (3), 1–9.

DesJarlais, D.C., Casriel, C., Stepherson, B. & Friedman, S. (1990) Expectations of racial prejudice in AIDS research and prevention programs in the United States. *Drugs and society, 5* (1/2), 1–7.

DiClemente, R. (Ed.). (1992). *Adolescents and AIDS: A generation in jeopardy.* Newbury Park, CA: Sage.

Draimin, B., Hudis, J. & Segura, J. (1992). *The mental health needs of well adolescents in families with AIDS*. New York City Human Resources Administration, Division of AIDS Services.

Durham, J. & Cohen, F. (1993). *Women, children, and HIV/AIDS*. New York: Springer.

Edelman, H. (1994). *Motherless daughters*. New York: Delta Publishing.

Ely, M., with Anzul, M., Friedman, T., Garner, D. & McCormick Steinmetz, A. (1991). *Doing qualitative research: Circles within circles*. London: The Falmer Press.

Ely, M., Vinz, R., Downing, M. & Anzul, M. (1997). *On writing qualitative research: Living by words*. Washington, DC: Falmer Press.

Ensminger. M. (1990). Sexual activity and problem behaviors among black, urban adolescents. *Child Development, 61*, 2032–2046.

Fernando, M. D. (1993). *AIDS and intravenous drug use: The influence of morality, politics, social science, and race in the making of a tragedy*. Westport, CT: Praeger.

Fitzpatrick, J. P. (1990). Drugs and Puerto Ricans in New York City. In Glick, R. & Moore, J. (Eds.). *Drugs in Hispanic Communities* (pp. 103–126). New Brunswick, NJ: Rutgers University Press.

Flora, J. & Thoresen, C. (1988). Reducing the risk of AIDS in adolescents. *American Psychologist, 43* (11), 965–970.

Flora, J. & Thoresen, C. (1989). Components of a comprehensive strategy for reducing the risk of AIDS in adolescents. In Mays, V., Albee, G. & Schneider, S. (Eds.). *Primary prevention of AIDS: Psychological approaches*. (pp. 374–389). Newbury Park, CA: Sage Publications.

Friedman, S. R., Sufian, M. & Des Jarlais, D. C. (1990). The AIDS epidemic among Latino intravenous drug users. In Glick, R. & Moore, J. (Eds.). *Drugs in Hispanic Communities* (pp. 45–54). New Brunswick, NJ: Rutgers University Press.

Gardner, W., Millstein, S. & Wilcox, B. (Eds.). (1990). *Adolescents in the AIDS epidemic*. San Francisco: Jossey-Bass.

Galea, R., Lewis, B. & Baker, L. (Eds.). (1988). *AIDS and IV drug abusers*. Owings Mills, MD: Rynd Communications.

Geballe, S., Gruendel, J. & Andiman, W. (Eds.). (1995). *Forgotten children of the AIDS epidemic*. New Haven CT: Yale University Press.

Groce, N. (1995). Children and AIDS in a multicultural perspective. In Geballe et al. *Forgotten Children of the AIDS Epidemic* (pp. 95–106). New Haven: Yale University Press.

Guba, E. & Lincoln, Y. (1981). *Effective evaluation*. San Francisco: Jossey-Bass.

Handelman, D. (1993). The new lost generation. *Vogue*. April, pp. 378, 380–382, 467–468.

Hayes, C. (1987). Determinants of adolescent sexual behavior and decision making. In Hayes, E. (Ed.). *Risking the future: Adolescent sexuality, pregnancy, and childbearing* (pp. 95–121). Washington, DC: National Academy Press.

Hein, K. (1990). Lessons from New York City on HIV/AIDS in adolescents. *New York State Journal of Medicine Special Issue: Acquired Immunodeficiency Syndromes, 90* (3), 143–145.

Henggeler, S., Melton, G. , & Rodrigue, J. (1992). *Pediatric and adolescent AIDS: Research findings from the social sciences.* Newbury Park, CA: Sage Publications.

Herdt, G., & Boxer, A. (1991). Ethnographic issues in the study of AIDS. *The Journal of Sex Research, 28* (2), 171–187.

Herek, G. & Glunt, E. (1988). An epidemic of stigma: Public reactions to AIDS. *American Psychologist, 43,* 886–891.

Hirshberg, C. (1995) The way we live: Gil. *Life.* September issue. pp. 50–58.

Hollander, S. (1995, August). *HIV /AIDS affected families: New demands, new responses.* Poster session presented at the annual meeting of the American Psychological Association, New York, NY.

Huber, J. & Schneider, B. (Eds.). (1992). *The social context of AIDS.* Newbury Park, CA: Sage Publications.

Hudis, J. (1995). Adolescents living in families with AIDS. In Geballe et al. (Eds.). *Forgotten children of the AIDS epidemic* (pp. 83–94). New Haven: Yale University Press.

Inclàn, J.E. & Herron, D.G. (1989). Puerto rican adolescents. In Gibbs, J. & Huang. L. (Eds.). *Children of color: Psychological intervention with minority youth* (pp. 251–277). CA: Jossey-Bass.

Irwin, C. & Millstein, S. (1991). Risk-taking behaviors during adolescence. In Lerner, R., Petersen, A. & Brooks-Gunn, J. (Eds.). *Encyclopedia of adolescence* (pp. 934–943). New York: Garland Publishing.

Johnson-Moore, P. & Phillips, L. (1994). Black American communities: Coping with death. In Dane, B. & Levine, C. (Eds.). *AIDS and the new orphans: Coping with death* (pp. 101–120). Westport, CT: Auburn House.

Jones, D. (1995, August). Coping and psychological well-being in individuals experiencing AIDS-related multiple loss. In Browning, C. (Chair), *Living, dying, and being left behind: Making sense of AIDS* . Symposium conducted at the annual meeting of the American Psychological Association, New York, NY.

Joseph, J., Emmons, E.A., Kessler, R., Wortman, C., O'Brien, K., Hocker, W. & Schaefer, C. (1984). Coping with the threat of AIDS: An approach to psychosocial assessment. *American Psychologist, 39* (11) 1297–1302.

Kalinoski, J. & Rothermel, C. (1995). Lessons from the street: Outreach to inner-city youth. *SIECUS Report, 23* (2), 14–17.

Kirby, D. (1984). *Sexuality education: Evaluation of programs and their effects.* Santa Cruz, CA: Network Publishing.

Kolata, G. (1993, March 7). Targeting urged in attack on AIDS. *New York Times,* pp. 1, 26.

Landers, S. (1989, November). AIDS stigma reaches epidemic proportions. *APA Monitor,* p. 5.

Levine, C. (1994). The new orphans and grieving in the time of AIDS. In Dane, B. & Levine, C. (Eds.). *AIDS and the new orphans: Coping with death* (pp. 1–12). Westport, CT: Auburn House.

Levine, C. & Stein, G. (1994). *Orphans of the HIV epidemic: Unmet needs of six U.S. cities.* New York: The Orphan Project.

Levine, C. (1990). AIDS and changing concepts of family. *Millbank Quarterly, 14,* 61–68.

Lewis, M. (1995). The special case of the uninfected child in the HIV affected family: Normal developmental tasks and the child's concerns about illness and death. In Geballe, S., Gruendel, J. & Andiman, W. (Eds.). *Forgotten children of the AIDS epidemic* (pp. 50–6). New Haven: Yale University Press.

Lincoln, Y, & Guba, E. (1985). *Naturalistic inquiry.* Newbury Park CA: Sage Publications.

Lofland, J. & Lofland, L. (1984). *Analyzing social settings: A guide to qualitative observation and analysis* (2nd ed.). Belmont, CA: Wadsworth Publishing Company.

Macklin, Eleanor. (Ed.). (1989). *AIDS and families.* New York: Harrington Park Press.

Martin, A.D. & Hetrick, E.S. (1987). Designing an AIDS risk reduction program for gay teenagers: Problems and proposed solutions. In Ostrow, D. (Ed.). *Biobehavioral control of AIDS* (pp. 137–152). New York: Irvington Publishers.

Mays, V. & Cochran, S. (1988). Issues in the perception of AIDS risk and risk reduction activities by black and Hispanic/Latina women. *American Psychologist, 43,* 949–957.

McKeganey, N. & Barnard, M. (1992). *AIDS, drugs and sexual risk: Lives in the balance.* Bristol, PA: Open University Press.

Mellins, C. A. (1995, August). The Impact of HIV disease on children and families. In L. Wicks (Chair), *HIV in the context of interpersonal and therapeutic relationships-Challenging assumptions.* Symposium conducted at the annual meeting of the American Psychological Association, New York, NY.

Morales, J. & Bok, M. (Eds.). (1992). *Multicultural human services for AIDS treatment and prevention: Policy perspectives and planning.* Binghamton, NY: Harrington Park Press.

Nagler, S., Adnopoz, J. & Forsyth, B. (1995) Uncertainty, stigma, and secrecy: Psychological aspects of AIDS for children and adolescents. In Geballe et al. (Eds.). *Forgotten children of the AIDS epidemic* (pp. 71–82). New Haven: Yale.

National Research Council. (1993). *The social impact of AIDS in the United States.* Washington, DC: National Academy Press.

Navarro, M. (1992, May 6). Left behind by AIDS. *New York Times.* p. B1, B10.

Needle, R., Leach, S. & Graham-Tomasi, R. (1989). The human immunodeficiency virus (HIV) epidemic: Epidemiological implications for family professionals. In Macklin, E. (Ed.). *AIDS and families* (pp. 13–37). New York: Harrington Park Press.

New York City Department of Health. (December, 1996). *AIDS New York City: AIDS surveillance update.* City of New York.

New York City Department of Health. (1997). *AIDS in boroughs & neighborhoods of New York City.* City of New York.

New York City Department of Health. (April, 1997). *AIDS New York City: AIDS surveillance update.* City of New York.

Novaco, R. (1979). Cognitive regulation of anger and stress. In Kendall, P. & Hollon, S. (Eds.). *Cognitive-behavioral interventions* (pp. 241–285). New York: Academic Press.

Patai, D. (1988). Constructing a self: A Brazilian life story. *Feminist Studies, 14* (1), 143–166.

Patierno, C. (1991). Children, adolescents and HIV/AIDS education: A SIECUS annotated bibliography. *SIECUS Report, 19* (2), 33–34.

Patton, M. (1980). *Qualitative evaluation methods.* Beverly Hills, CA: Sage Publications.

Pizzo, P. & Wilfert, C. (Eds.). (1994). *Pediatric AIDS: The challenge of HIV infection in infants, children, and adolescents* (2nd ed.). Baltimore, MD: Williams & Wilkins.

Rait, D. (1991). The family context of AIDS. *Psychiatric Medicine, 9* (3), 423–437.

Richardson, L. (1998, January 2). When AIDS steals a parent. *New York Times,* pp. B1, B6.

Rotheram-Borus, M.J. (1995, August). Adolescents whose parents have AIDS: Reducing risk behavior and coping with disclosure. In R. Diclemente (Chair), *HIV and AIDS-Recruitment and intervention for adolescents and families.* Symposium conducted at the annual meeting of the American Psychological Association, New York, NY.

Rotheram-Borus, M. J. & Koopman, C. (1991). AIDS and adolescents. In Lerner, R., Peterson, J. & Brooks-Gunn, J. (Eds.). *The encyclopedia of adolescence* (pp. 29–36). New York: Garland Publishing.

Rotheram-Borus, M. J. & Koopman, C. (1992). Adolescents. In Stuber, M. (Ed.). *Children and AIDS.* (pp. 45–68). Washington, DC: American Psychiatric Press.

Rotheram-Borus, M. J., Koopman, C. & Bradley, J. (1988, June). Barriers to successful AIDS prevention programs with runaway youth. In *Issues in prevention and treatment of AIDS among adolescents with serious emotional disturbance.* Paper presented at the Knowledge Development Workshop, Georgetown University Child Development Center, Washington, DC.

Sexuality Information and Education Council of the United States. (1997). Fact sheet on sexually transmitted diseases in the United States. *SIECUS Report, 25* (3), 22–24.

Siebert, J. & Olson, R. (Eds.). (1989). *Children, adolescents, & AIDS.* Lincoln, NE: University of Nebraska Press.

Sontag, D. & Richardson, L. (1997, March 2). Doctors withhold H.I.V. pill regimen from some. *The New York Times,* pp. A1, A35.

Spradley, J. (1979). *The ethnographic interview.* Orlando, FL: Holt, Rinehart and Winston.

St. Louis, M., Conway, G., Hayman, C., Miller, C., Petersen, L. & Dondero, T. (1991). Human immunodeficiency virus infection in disadvantaged adolescents: Findings from the US Job Corps, *Journal of the American Medical Association, 266* (17), 2387–2391.

Strauss, A. (1987). *Qualitative analysis for social scientists.* New York: Cambridge University Press.

Teltsch, K. (1991, August 27). Mothers dying of AIDS get child custody help. *New York Times,* pp B1, B4.

Tiblier, K., Walker, G. & Rolland, J. (1989). Therapeutic issues when working with families of persons with AIDS. In Macklin, E. (Ed.). *AIDS and families.* Binghamton, NY: Harrington Park Press.

Wallace, R. (1988). A synergism of plagues: "Planned shrinkage," contagious housing destruction, and AIDS in the Bronx. *Environmental Research, 47,* 1–33.

Wolcott, H. (1990). *Writing up qualitative research.* Newbury Park, CA: Sage Publications.

Yondorf, B. (1990). Adolescents and AIDS: Stopping the time bomb. *State Legislative Report, 15* (12).

Zayas, L. & Romano, K. (1994) Adolescents and parental death from AIDS. In Dane, B. & Levine, C. (Eds.). *AIDS and the new orphans: Coping with death* (pp. 59–76). Westport, CT: Auburn House.

Zimet, G., Hillier, S., Anglin, T., Ellich, E., Krowchuk, D. & Williams, P. (1991). Knowing someone with AIDS: The impact on adolescents. *Journal of Pediatric Psychology, 16* (3), 287–294.

Index